ON THE SOCIOLOGY OF KNOWLEDGE
an essay

INTRODUCTION BY *Robert M. MacIver*
CHANCELLOR,
THE NEW SCHOOL FOR SOCIAL RESEARCH

On the Sociology of Knowledge

an essay by Hans Neisser

PROFESSOR, GRADUATE FACULTY
THE NEW SCHOOL FOR SOCIAL RESEARCH

James H. Heineman, Inc., New York H

First Printing 1965
Library of Congress Catalogue Card Number: 64–23626

For information address: James H. Heineman, Inc., 60 East 42nd Street, New York, New York 10017.
Printed and bound in the United States of America

BY THE SAME AUTHOR:

The Exchange Value of Money
Some International Aspects of the Business Cycle
National Income and International Trade
(in collaboration with Modigliani)

To Adolph Lowe
on the occasion of his 70th Birthday

Contents

II *The procedural rules of nonexperimental science*

III *History as social science*

PREFACE

The approach of this essay is systematic. I have no desire to give a survey of the literature, but wish rather to discuss the problems and to hint at their solutions. I believe that the first task of anyone writing on the sociology of knowledge is to state what he means by "knowledge." Even the brief investigation in my first chapter shows that the best known among my predecessors had dealt with only a part of knowledge, as this term is usually understood. Hence, legitimate problems of a sociology of knowledge had not been touched upon.

The attempt to widen the scope of the investigation to cover knowledge as it is generally understood led me in Chapter 3 to discuss questions usually treated in general sociology and history. I was therefore forced to rely, to a great extent, on secondary sources.

It may seem inconsistent that, in turning to historical-ideological knowledge, I temporarily abandoned the systematic approach and used the formulations of Karl Mannheim as a starting point. There were two reasons for this procedure. First, in the United States Mannheim is considered to be the leading exponent in this field. I refer the reader, for example, to the authority of R. K. Merton,[1] to whose surprisingly favorable summary of Mannheim's achievement I am, however, unable to subscribe. The sec-

[1] R. K. Merton, *Social Theory and Social Structure,* Ch. IX.

ond reason is the immanent development in Mannheim's thought, particularly noticeable in his posthumous writings, which his critics were not able to consult and which, in my opinion, point in the right direction.

As for Mannheim's predecessors, Marx and Engels have been discussed *ad nauseam;* their exposition is extremely brief, and I was able to limit myself to some comments in the appendix to this essay. Durkheim's formulations have been submitted to a thorough analysis by Merton and by H. O. Dahlke.[2] Max Scheler's *Die Wissenformen und die Gesellschaft* has a metaphysical orientation and could not be discussed here without taking up almost all of the principal questions of philosophy. Other philosophical approaches have been subjected to a trenchant criticism by Arthur Child.[3]

In developing systematically the problems of the sociology of knowledge, I was, at a certain point, forced to discuss basic methodological questions of the nonexperimental sciences to an extent which, contrary to my original intentions, makes this short volume an essay in the methodology of the social sciences. I can only hope that I have succeeded in sketching intelligibly the common content of the various approaches, exclusive of the extreme schools. As to the method actually applied in scientific work, the difference between Neo-Positivism, Neo-Kantianism, and phenomenology is not nearly so great as the difference in terminology would make it appear to many readers.

In one respect, however, the differences between the schools remain substantial, namely, in the question: Is there any reason to treat the human mind as a passive and merely recording instrument? In a sense, this ques-

[2] H. O. Dahlke, "The Sociology of Knowledge," in H. E. Barnes, *Contemporary Social Theory.*

[3] Arthur Child, "The Theoretical Possibility of the Sociology of Knowledge," in *Ethics,* vol. 57 (1940-41), esp. p. 393.

tion permeates the whole history of philosophy, and I cannot blame the reader who finds my remarks in Chapter 2 superficial. On the other hand, it seemed impossible to proceed in a systematic discussion of the sociology of knowledge without stating clearly my position on this point.

The principal aim of this essay is clarification. There is a certain type of philosophical-sociological writing which is utterly foreign to me and which has no place here. To quote Arthur Child (*op. cit.*, p. 412): "If it can be established that both in origin and constitution the mind is ineluctably social, then there will remain no doubt that knowledge is, in some sense and to some degree, expressive of a social determination." The reader who expects insights of this nature should stop at this point.[N.B.]

N.B. I wish to gratefully acknowledge the valuable suggestions of my colleagues, Hans Staudinger and Dennis Wrong, regarding the contents of this essay, and to thank Miss F. Rosenwald, Mrs. H. Neisser, and Mr. W. Freeman for the assistance given at various times in editing.

INTRODUCTION

"The principal aim of this essay is clarification." So Dr. Neisser informs us at the outset, and he admirably fulfills his aim. It is the most clear-sighted study I have read on a subject that has considerable significance but has not received the thorough analysis it calls for. The first of many questions we have to ask is this: What kinds or aspects of knowledge do we refer to when we think of them as in one way or another affected by social conditions? We might place at one end of the scale mathematical formulations, on the construction of which social conditions—social position or social influences of any kind—play no perceptible role, and at the other end history and the social sciences, which are certainly in various ways affected by the changing social climate. If, however, we refine our question to include the various modes in which knowledge, as distinct from mere opinion or doctrines determined by authority or by tradition, is affected by social considerations, it will appear that the range open to the sociology of knowledge is most extensive.

Let us frame our question as follows: In what respects, if any, does one form of knowledge or another tend to be (1) influenced in its content or conclusions by the ideology of the group, (2) affected in its growth or direction by the immediate interests or temporary passions of the group, without specific relation to its ideology, (3) limited in its scope or character by the ideology or specific interests of the group? Under the third division, as the history of science amply illustrates, the whole range of subjects from astronomy to psychology have been blocked by the dogmatic assumptions of theology or other ideological preconceptions. In the Soviet Union the study of genetics has been warped by Marxist pronouncements and the famous "monkey" trial in Tennessee is still recent history.

Such broad considerations are but the starting point for the more subtle and interesting questions pertaining to the sociology of knowledge that Dr. Neisser so competently analyzes in this study. Man is the knower, the sapient one—to a degree low or higher, but his knowing is crossed by the worship of the various idols Francis Bacon enumerated. The quest for knowledge, however sincere, has its obstacles and its pitfalls, and faced with these difficulties the mind slides easily along the line of prepossessions from inadequate observation to insecure deduction and from the fact of sequence to the shaky attribution of cause.

We cannot in the brief foreword comment on the many ways in which Dr. Neisser develops his own approach to the controversial aspects of his theme, but we found particularly helpful his treatment of economics as a social science and of history and its basic problems. As his work proceeds it becomes a short and effective discussion of scientific methodology, for, as he puts it, the adherence to scientific method is the sure way in which science advances and "makes the investigation relatively free from prejudice."

Robert M. MacIver
March, 1965

SYNOPSIS

By sociology of knowledge we may understand two different types of investigation. First, are there particular social conditions which have obstructed or furthered, and will continue to obstruct or further, the development of knowledge? Second, is the content of the statements of an individual or of the leaders of a cohesive social group determined by the social situation?

Since the first question has been somewhat neglected in the literature, and, since knowledge as usually understood does not mean modern science alone, we shall devote a lengthy chapter to the sociology of *practical* knowledge. Even here an important difference in our approach from the position of the founders of the sociology of knowledge, Marx and Engels, and its leading representative in our century, Mannheim, will become visible: the development of knowledge cannot be adequately understood, if we deny to the human mind any urge, however faint, to enrich itself; thus intellectual history is governed by an *interpenetration* of social factors and autonomous tendencies of the human mind. This viewpoint allowed us to discuss from a new angle the question why the experimental sciences in the modern sense of the term developed only within one civilization and even here rather late. When the magical interpretation of events outside the power of man was once abandoned, it was not science, as we understand it today, but primarily speculation which took the place of magic; and then the social factors obstructed rather than promoted the further development. It needed a peculiar concatenation of empirical tendencies to overcome the block which, e.g., in Chinese civilization, obstructed the rise of experimental science.

This short summary already confirms what the investigation in our opinion will show: that the sociology of knowledge is itself a *historical science,* in the sense that the influence of social factors on the development of knowledge has undergone and will continue to undergo historical changes. There is no simple formula which answers the question posed by the sociology of knowledge. This point will become particularly clear when we shall study the various formulae in which Mannheim tried to present in a nutshell his sociology of historical-ideological knowledge. Once and for all, such attempts should be given up; a "technological conception" of history is no better than the materialistic conception, concerning which some remarks can be found in the appendix.

The study of Mannheim yields an answer to the question: If the content of knowledge depends on the social position of the "assertor," how can we explain that human knowledge, outside the science of nature and mathematics, has made and may make any progress? Our conclusion is that method, following rules of procedure of science, makes the investigator relatively free of prejudices, a conclusion foreshadowed in Mannheim's posthumous work.

The second part of this essay, therefore, is devoted to a sketch of these rules of procedure for the nonexperimental sciences. The presuppositions and the limitations of the statistical method will prove to be the core of these rules. Economic models will represent the starting point, and the question of a total social model is discussed at the end of the chapter of sociology.

What if the presuppositions of the statistical method are not satisfied, if the material is inadequate, and the defects become serious? If this happens in the science of nature, e.g. meteorology, the research worker will unhesitatingly confess his inability to give an answer; the rules of procedure are deeply ingrained in his intellect and do not easily allow prejudices from other fields of his mind to invade his special work. If he yields to temptation, he will be called to order by his colleagues. In the systematic sciences of economics and sociology the rules have been formulated, explicitly or implicitly, only during the last 100 years, and traces of the "ideologies" of the 18th and 19th century are still visible. Here it has not proved easy to clarify completely the relation between the concepts of science and the events of social reality, especially since the complexity of reality made far reaching simplifications ("idealizations") unavoidable.

While the systematic social sciences have made regular progress in liberating themselves from the ideologies, historiography has encountered almost insuperable difficulties, as we shall try to show in the third part of this essay. In the absence of a total social model, the historian all too frequently has been satisfied with explaining events on the basis of a hastily constructed model of his own, in which, consciously or subconsciously, he accepted the ideology of the class in which he grew up, or to which he attached himself. The instinctive aversion of the social scientist to discussing the problems of the social order, which persisted until the end of the 18th century, as discussed in the last chapter, is only one of the numerous expressions of this ideology. While the master of modern historiography, Ranke, was protected against such a naïve ideological interpretation by the instinctive self-criticism of his genius, it was his most important contribution to method, namely, the source-critique, that fostered naïve interpretations. For a long time, if not forever, historiography will remain the field which a critical sociology of knowledge will have to watch most carefully.

PART I

Basic problems

1

KNOWLEDGE

The sociology of knowledge, as presented in the writings of Karl Mannheim, refers only to a particular brand of knowledge, which, for lack of a better term, we shall call historical-ideological knowledge. "Historical" refers here to history as it has been generally written—in other words, to a historiography which has rarely satisfied the strict criteria which we will discuss in Part II of this essay. The term "ideological" in the sense used here was first introduced by Marx and Engels as the name of the philosophical-political systems which tried to justify, by derivation from general principles, a particular political position. It was soon extended to cover the political positions of large social groups, or rather the positions held by the great majority of the members of these groups. Marx would call ideological a statement such as the following: "I am a landowner and therefore a free-trader." As we shall see, Mannheim's use of these and similar terms was not so clear as one might wish.

Mannheim apparently did not include in the sociology of knowledge such techniques as the philological technique, the historical technique of "source-critique," or the juridical technique of interpreting the law, although, in fact there had been some controversy between the adherents of the traditional and the sociological technique of interpretation. He expressly exempted mathematics and natural science. His attitude to the social science of his own time is not clear. Marx and Engels also exempted mathematics and natural science, though they certainly included the political economy of their time.

Neither Mannheim nor his predecessors or critics showed any interest in what we shall call the sociology of "practical knowledge," although that knowledge was the only knowledge of mankind (*homo sapiens,* including Neanderthal man) for about two hundred thousand years, and despite the fact that the basic advances of technology in industrial capitalism up to the middle of the nineteenth century were in the field of practical knowledge and were not due to the application of modern science. We denote by the term "practical knowledge" the human know-how that is not based on a systematic knowledge of the laws governing nature or society but, though obtained pragmatically, possesses a high degree of certainty: for example, how to till the soil, how to make simple tools, how to care for a herd, how to hunt. Knowledge of certain basic regularities of nature (day and night, seasonal changes, etc.) is another example. On the other hand, the acquisition of personal skills is excluded. Thus, inventing the long bow represents an addition to practical knowledge, but learning its use is not such an addition.[4] The stress on certainty is designed to exclude magical knowledge. Once obtained, practical knowledge usually established a tradition which, except in the last centuries, proved a serious obstacle to its further development.

There is good reason for the exclusion of this type of

[4] It goes without saying, that even after 1600 A.D., when modern science arose, mankind added to its practical knowledge. It is one of the merits of M. T. Pledge, *Science Since 1500* (1939), especially p. 154, to have made clear that the great scholars of the Renaissance—a Leonardo, an Agricola—belong to the history of practical knowledge and are not the precursors of science proper. *See also:* A. Koyré, "Galileo and Plato," *Journal of the History of Ideas* (October 1943), p. 405, footnote 13.

knowledge from the sociology of knowledge. Since about 3000 B.C., practical knowledge has been reflected in the institutions and, more generally, in the social relations of the age, and the sociology of knowledge would, to that extent, fuse with sociology in general, in its systematic and its historical aspects.[5] Nevertheless, we shall not completely neglect it, but, by way of illustration, will show that some problems in general sociology could be approached advantageously from the viewpoint of the sociology of knowledge. We find it equally impossible to disregard the sociology of natural science, because of the affinity of some of its methods to those of "modern" social science. We shall further find that among the latter, the writing on history holds a separate position.

On the other hand, we exclude from the concept of knowledge, as used here, unorganized random talk and also the observation of current events and the information about them transmitted by the observer to other people, so-called protocol statements, though they represent the basis of empirical knowledge. This is a more serious decision than may appear at first glance, because the transition from these statements to a mere description of parts of the world or historical events is gradual; and description is the indispensable basis[6] of explanation and prediction by laws, and of the relation of cause and effect.[6a] In history, pure description has become rare in-

[5] The fusion of sociology of knowledge and general sociology would have been even more pronounced had we tried to deal with all problems which Talcott Parsons in his Introduction to Part IV of *Theories of Society*, vol. II, p. 991, outlined for the former. His second task is to examine the conditions for practical implementation of scientific knowledge (plus, we assume, of the degree of willingness to learn). Tasks 1 and 3 will be briefly discussed at the end of this essay.

[6] In this sense, Darwin praises the scholarship of Aristotle and Cuvier, the latter being the most outspoken foe of the theory of evolution.

[6a] Methodologically there is a difference between the formulation of such laws and the explanation in terms of cause and

deed, but it would be pedantic to deny to a historical work the quality of being descriptive because it makes use of some noncontroversial laws of nature. But how difficult it is even for the "descriptive" historian to avoid slipping over into controversial explanation is shown, for example, by the cause-effect chain which a Chinese historian might have written: drought—starvation—rebellion against the ruler. The first link refers to an uncontroversial law of nature; the second is a sociological explanation and requires proof.

We do not wish to deny that both the ability and the desire to observe and to describe have undergone historical changes, in which conceivably social factors were active, though probably magic and tradition had a stronger influence. We have not devoted a separate study to description because the sociological problems in description and explanation are not basically different. In particular, description, like history, requires some kind of selection. The contrary idea of M. Oakeshott that history gives a full account of change and that this full account can replace the conception of cause and explanation clearly requires something which is not possible.[7]

The description, in this case, is in terms of daily life. There are other forms of expression, however. The protocol statements of an experimenter may describe observations in terms of mere perception. The description of the state of not directly observable entities like magnetic fields uses technical concepts, and is possible only by inference; hence it presupposes a definition of those concepts in terms of observables. Note that the term "construct" for these entities is misleading, because it implies an inferior kind of reality. However, the ordinary things

---

effect, though of course, the latter depends on the former. For the present purpose the distinction can be neglected. It will be discussed in Chapter 9.

[7] M. Oakeshott, *Experience and Its Modes*, p. 143.

of life, like a tree or a house, would then be constructs, too. Nobody has ever seen the front and the back of a tree at the same time, but seeing the front and realizing that one sees a tree, one can make anticipatory statements about the back—"constructing" it.

The reader will also notice that the religious experience is not considered as knowledge, nor do we regard other acts of a purely emotional character as belonging to this category. We need not assure the reader that in excluding these mental acts from knowledge we do not deny their vast effects on the development of the human mind; they have formed practical knowledge, and they may appear as forces in the "model," which we consider the basic tool of nonexperimental sciences.

The extension of the concept of a sociology of knowledge beyond Mannheim and Marx-Engels adds new questions, too. In addition to their central question of whether the content of human knowledge is influenced by the social environment of the "assertor," we shall also consider the extent to which the development of human knowledge has been conditioned by the social environment. It will be seen that these two questions refer to entirely different problems.

Lastly, we have to answer the question whether, in the social factors that affect and possibly determine knowledge, knowledge itself is contained as presupposition. In principle, we must answer the question in the affirmative. The social framework has, as one building block, some results of practical knowledge, and, at least since the middle of the nineteenth century, science in the modern sense has affected the framework. At no time, however, has knowledge been the only building block. Psychological elements like emotion and desire, the influence of belief in magic, and the freezing of genuine knowledge into tradition have all played a large role in erecting the framework. But even apart from these other influences, the appearance of knowledge in the social framework does not involve the sociologist in circular thinking. The knowledge that is retained as building block in the social framework is a part of acquired knowledge, that is, knowledge obtained on a historical stage in the past. The problem treated by the sociology of knowledge is, therefore: Does the social framework, including the knowledge built into it, influence the further development of knowledge—and how?

2

THE AUTONOMY OF THE HUMAN MIND

In his article, "*Sociology of Knowledge,* Karl Mannheim identifies the sociology of knowledge as a special, methodologically well-founded branch of sociology with the fact that thought is existentially determined. "The existential determination of thought may be regarded as a demonstrated fact in those realms of thought in which we can show (a) that the process of knowing does not actually develop historically in accordance with immanent laws, that it does not follow only from the 'nature of things' or from 'pure logical possibilities' and that it is not driven by an 'inner dialectic' . . . . This existential determination of thought will also have to be regarded as a fact (b) if the influence of these existential factors on the concrete content of knowledge is of more than peripheral importance, if they are relevant not only to the genesis of ideas, but penetrate into their forms and content and if, furthermore, they decisively determine the scope and the intensity of our experience and observation. . . ." [8]

The reader will note that these two conditions are neither interdependent, nor logically or epistemologically complementary. On the contrary, it is possible to agree with (a) without conceding (b) in the particular form

[8] Karl Mannheim, "Sociology of Knowledge," in *Ideology and Utopia,* Part V. This part was published originally in a German encyclopedia of sociology, and will be quoted as S.K. article.

stated by Mannheim. Here we wish to say a few words about the problem of the "immanent" (autonomous, independent) development of the human mind. We have to side with Mannheim if we take his formulation literally, but are dissatisfied with a formulation which could be understood as denying the historical character of the human mind.

The position that the human mind produces thought according to some immanent philosophical law is usually attributed to Hegel. One could, for example, consider the empiricism of British philosophy from Bacon to Hume as the antithesis of the rationalism which dominated the Continent from Descartes to Leibniz and Wolff and the Enlightenment, and find the synthesis in Kant's *Critique of Pure Reason.* This example, however, cannot be found in Hegel's Lectures on the History of Philosophy.[9]

More to the point is the fact that the typical histories of philosophy, so far as they are known to the present writer, have a tendency to contrast the writings of successive philosophers and philosophical schools, as if they had originated exclusively in the desire of an author to dispute his predecessor. The same is true, in general, for the history of natural science, though Mach in his justly famous historical account of mechanics mentions the significance of the "material civilization," meaning the machines and tools handed down from generation to generation.[10] Thus, even in Mach, the separation of the history of ideas from the social matrix of the thinker would still be complete.

But though we grant Mannheim the error committed in this separation and, like him, deny the immanence in

[9] In the third part of the Lectures, Hegel's main interest is clearly to show the elements of the correctly understood "Philosophy of Identity" in his great idealistic predecessors. (See, for example, his subsection on Descartes or the last two paragraphs on Kant.)

[10] Ernst Mach, *The Science of Mechanics,* Ch. I, Sect. V, p. 104 (1942). This is a translation of the 9th German edition.

the development of human thinking, we have to point out some essential aspects of the development which in his formulation (a) are likely to get lost. Our first point, we are reasonably sure, would not have been denied by Mannheim, but we need to make it as the basis of the second point.

Obviously, knowledge is always particular in the sense that it is not the total of human knowledge available. This is true even in the extreme case (which, outside of mathematics, has never been realized) that the total of knowledge can be derived from a few axioms, and, in this sense, is implied by them; for the always limited power of the human brain, geniuses not excluded, prevents the mind from surveying the total in one glance. Some correct statements could not be made unless others had been made before and had been made available to the human being who discovers new truth, or who learns it later by rote. One has to be careful in giving illustrations: although Newton's calculus of fluxions, according to his own statement, represents a vast generalization of Fermat's tangent method of finding the maxima and minima of a function, it is not only possible that Newton might have developed the calculus without a knowledge of Fermat, but the order of presentation in our textbooks shows that the logic of the calculus can precede its application to the theory of maxima and minima. But calculus without a preceding development of elementary algebra is an impossibility. Or to take an example from natural science: the dynamo could not have been developed before the relation between electrical current and mechanical movement had been established by Faraday's experiments. Clearly, in the field of practical knowledge, it would not have been possible to build an ancient trireme (three-bench galley) before one had learned to make a small boat to cross a quiet river.

To proceed in our second point, this immanent, though

somewhat tenuous, temporal order in the development of the human mind has a peculiarity that will prove important for other reflections. This historical relation is something which can be ascertained and recorded ex post facto, but it does not change the fact that the productivity of the human mind visible ex post is unpredictable. It is, of course, possible to make negative predictions. For instance, no mental product like Newton's *Principia* could have materialized in 1686 A.D. among the Bushmen. This is very trivial sociology of knowledge. But even if we limit ourselves to the problem of the immanence of the development of the human mind (no calculus before algebra), we notice the philosophically remarkable fact that no mathematician, though in full possession of algebra, not even Fermat himself, could have predicted Newton's *Principia,* for predicting them would have been equivalent to writing them, or rather to working out their essential ideas.

We choose the latter formulation for two reasons: (1) to show that intellectual developments are sometimes anticipated as an unproven surmise, which is not identical with "working them out," or at least their "style" is predicted [11] and (2) to counter the argument that no prediction ever refers to all details of the predicted event. In the example given, it is not the details that could not have been predicted, but the essentials.

Retrospectively, however, the historian can establish immanent relations. Studying a particular time, he may note that a cultural development, known to him as existing in different times or a different civilization, failed, because of the social environment or for other reasons,

[11] As for the "style" of the future intellectual product, we should remember (what Mannheim in his favorite comparison between intellectual history and history of art overlooks) that the style changes from time to time, and that, to the best of this writer's knowledge, no prediction of such changes has ever been attempted.

to materialize in the time under consideration, though it was implied in the actual knowledge of the time. For example, Archimedes' work contained the unripened seed for the development of the integral calculus. Thus, every stage of development is a matrix of possible further progress. The point we are making here will be generalized in our discussion of history as social science. (Part III)

What is immanent in our approach is not the specific development of the human mind which by itself could explain intellectual history, but a certain "faint urge" of the mind to go ahead. That, by itself, outside of specific historical stages of development, the urge is faint will be seen in the following chapter. But though faint, it is never nil; and if under favorable circumstances it grows stronger, it displays peculiar marks which cannot be explained by the circumstances. Intellectual history must, therefore, be conceived as an interpenetration of social-historical factors and the autonomy of the human mind.

3

SOME PROBLEMS OF THE SOCIOLOGY OF PRACTICAL KNOWLEDGE

A) Early phases

Apeman and paleolithic man possessed skills that they could not have acquired without some thinking. Knowledge begins in this period at the latest. We do not know enough of this period to answer questions about the influence of the social environment on the development of this knowledge, but there are some facts that are scarcely disputed.

First, the practical knowledge of paleolithic man depended on the physical-geographical conditions in which he lived. Second, during the greater part of the history of man, including or excluding the Neanderthaler, he remained at the level of hunting and food gathering, using extremely primitive tools. Domestication of animals and agriculture, even in primitive forms, preceded the highly developed civilizations of Sumer and Egypt by only a few thousand years. Third, there are some devices, simple but important, and rarely known to primitive tribes, which first appeared in the Bronze Age, or in what are known as higher civilizations; for example, the wheel which appeared in Sumer between 3500 and 2750 B.C. It is possible that the uncivilized Indo-European charioteers, who overran in the second millennium, a large part of the world from India to Greece and Egypt, took over the wheel from a higher civilization.

Finally, if we consider the enormous span of time

through which paleolithic man lived, we must conclude that either the spirit of innovation was extremely rare, or that the social obstacles to innovation inherent in tradition or a belief in magic were almost insuperable. The latter hypothesis gains weight from the fact that the interpretation of the noncontrollable forces of nature around man was, indeed, based on magic; and magic, once crystallized into a system and ritual, is a severe obstacle to many innovations. But the first alternative is not excluded by the fact because the "rarity" hypothesis can be supported by observations from historical times.

As an illustration, let us refer to the art of horseback riding known in the Mediterranean area at least since 700 B.C. The earliest report is of the Persian-Iranian horse (the only one which survived throughout ancient times); then the Macedonian-Thessalic cavalry which broke the Greek phalanx; the *equites* of ancient Rome (who were financiers in historical times and did not ride); the Numidean horse, which first helped Hannibal to win his victories and then defeated him; and the Gallic warriors of Caesar's time, apparently all feudalized and, in contrast to the warriors of the battle at Allia, fighting as cavalry.[12] Although this art had flourished for about a thousand years, the use of the stirrup remained unknown until it was taken over from Asiatic tribes in the fourth century. No magical-ritualistic forces are known which could have prevented this simple invention from materializing.

This example also proves that it is not simple need that provokes innovation,[13] and that "challenge and response" are not general categories that truly explain any development, as the cause-effect relation claims to do. Many

[12] In Caesar's time the Germanic youth knew how to ride bareback and helped to win the battle of Pharsalus, but the bulk of the Germanic warriors fought on foot.

[13] In the technological age in which we live, "need" in a specific sense creates to some extent its own fulfillment.

challenges had no response, or only one of many possible responses. In general, the human race seems to have been satisfied for millennia with elementary adjustments required for survival. The development of the last centuries is the exception and is the result of a cultural transformation. In possession of the art of fire-making and some simple tools, primitive man, whether hunter, nomad, or small peasant, could satisfy his basic "instinctive" needs. He could even, utilizing the experience of a hundred thousand years, treat a great number of the ailments to which man is apparently more susceptible than his predecessors; a considerable number of folk medicines, by no means entirely useless, date back to times before the rise of civilizations. Most of the ailments that primitive man could not handle, mankind did not learn to treat (apart from some surgical-obstetrical progress) till about the middle of the nineteenth century.

B) Later phases of practical knowledge

Whereas for early times the sociology of knowledge is a part of anthropology, it merges with sociology in general and with history in later phases. The problems are represented by the extension of knowledge, which was associated with town life and the city economy (by no means a general development) and the transition from the city-state to a system of commercial capitalism, which presumably covered the world beyond the still primitive regions. In actual fact, however, several world economies unrelated and unknown to each other existed at the same time (e.g., the Chinese and the Mediterranean civilization around 100 A.D.). It appears that the second transition from the city economy to commercial capitalism was a general phenomenon, except where the former was prematurely destroyed by outside influences, as in the case of the city-state of the Aztecs wiped out by the Spanish invasion.[14]

These transitions could not have been possible without the development of new types of military and political organization. The military organization had to be based not only on some new knowledge, but on special leadership qualities, in line with Napoleon's dictum, on a balance of insight and power of resolution. There must have been an extension of practical knowledge wherever the short-run predatory invasions of neighboring tribes were replaced by the migration of the tribes ending in "Ueberlagerung" (subjugation or at least penetration of an indigenous population by invading groups).[15]

The expansion of knowledge, indispensable to the transition to the city, consisted of (1) improving architectural skills (from the tent or hut to the house and the city wall) (2) improving primitive arithmetical proficiency and (3) acquiring the art of some kind of record-keeping. The transition to commercial capitalism required primarily the aggrandizement of what the previous stage had already achieved.[16] It further allowed a degree of specialization which for markets of smaller size is unattainable. The most important novelty was probably the extension

[14] The transition to the universal state, so much stressed by Toynbee, was not performed by the one "universal" or "world" economy which is the most interesting of all, namely, the Western world economy which emerged between 1100 and 1300 A.D.

[15] It has not yet been fully proved that "subjugation" was a necessary condition for the rise of higher civilizations, in whatever size or political form, but it seems to have been the case at least in the vast majority of instances; it was achieved only in the minority of cases by horseback riders and primarily by charioteers (around 1500 B.C.) or warriors on foot; in addition, there was peaceful penetration like the Aramaic penetration of Syria and large parts of Mesopotamia.

[16] The change in quantity sometimes generates a qualitative change. Improved arithmetic proficiency and record-keeping becomes bookkeeping and writing.

of the use of money[17] which, even if known in earlier periods, could become general only when the improvement of transportation made large markets possible and opened the way to speculative financial activities comparable to those of our times.

The sociology of knowledge of these phases must answer the following questions:

1) How was the expansion of knowledge generated? We definitely do not have enough material to answer the question conclusively. However, let us recall that the spirit of innovation under primitive conditions is rare and meets severe obstacles. On the other hand, the social pressures making for the tribal exodus put a certain premium on the innovation in question: in this case, need plus chance generated progress, and a single success of this kind would, through imitation, facilitate other attempts.[18]

2) As has been pointed out, the transition from the city-state to the quasi-universal state was much more general and undertaken after a relatively short period of time. The sociologist will, therefore, be inclined to ascribe a particular role to the mere fact of agglomeration and social stratification, which was not necessarily brought about by subjugation. The city-state has not only master

[17] Charlemagne's famous monetary reform, which still survives in the pound sterling, the shilling, and the penny, could not prevent Europe north of the Alps from remaining for three centuries a feudal economy based not on money taxes but on tributes in kind.

[18] The pressures would be of physical origin like climatic changes or of Malthusian nature (low infant mortality), combined in the non-agricultural tribes with the boredom of a plethora of male youth not fully employed. The last-mentioned combination explains only intertribal raids and feuds. This writer has always been at a loss to understand the motives for the migration of the East Germanic tribes in the fourth century A.D. Roman wealth would not have lured the Gothic tribes to the shores of the Black Sea. Was it the barrier of the West German tribes which deflected the path of the East Germans?

builders and record keepers; it has a ruling class, which usually includes the custodians of the magic and ritual. In this class, from time to time, there appear leaders who not only aspire to expansion but see the way to achieve it —a way, as we have noted, that does not require a particularly original extension of practical knowledge. The similarities in the development of practical knowledge arise from the structural necessities of an international commercial capitalism. The differences arise (except for physical-geographical reasons) from the chance element in the history of the human mind. How can it be otherwise explained that double accounting developed only in the late Middle Ages and not during the Hellenistic-Roman era after 100 B.C.?

3) A negative result remains to be explained: the failure of all but one of the higher civilizations, endowed as they were with the practical knowledge required by commercial capitalism, to develop industrial capitalism—in other words, to improve systematically the methods of production. This is not the same as asking how modern science came into being, because for centuries industrial capitalism did not, and could not, make use of the progress of science proper.

The error of considering industrial capitalism a product of modern experimental science is committed even by economic historians and is probably due to the fact that both date back to about 1600 A.D. However, Watt's invention of the steam engine antedates Carnot's basic law of thermodynamics by about forty years. And what, we may ask, was the influence of modern physics from Galileo to Lagrange on industrial technique, or that of Boyle on what are called the chemical industries of the seventeenth and eighteenth centuries? [19] As late as the middle of the nine-

[19] It is worth noting that modern experimental science arose in a Catholic environment and even for the 18th century it would be difficult to show any superiority of Protestantism in this re-

teenth century, British engineers rejected as "scientific humbug" the suggestion of the Siemens brothers that cables be scientifically tested before they were laid.[20]

C) *Practical knowledge in industrial capitalism*

Industrial capitalism. Industrial capitalism is a system of production in which the average output per worker (or per man-hour) increases with a certain regularity. This increase is *primarily* due to the "vertical" division of labor, in which each worker performs only a part of the processing of the material and hands the semi-processed merchandise to another worker who continues the processing until the last worker in the chain delivers the fully processed material for sale. As a *second* criterion we could adduce the replacement of human manpower by tamed natural forces: very old is the use of wind power and water power, but precisely because it is very old, this replacement cannot be used as criterion for the transition of commercial to industrial capitalism at the end of the Middle Ages. The difference from the use of steam power, electricity and so on, which indeed represent a *caesura* in industrial capitalism, lies in the fact that these forces are *generally* applicable. It follows already from these definitions that the mere massing of workers in an ergasterion is not industrial capitalism; we have to exclude likewise

---

spect. The frequently cited "opposition" of the Catholic church to the Copernican system, and later to Darwin, was of very short duration; as far as we know the teaching of the theory of evolution is still forbidden in Baptist Tennessee, but not forbidden in any Catholic country. As for the "chemical" industries of these centuries, see Werner Sombart, *Modern Capitalism* II, 2, Ch. 46, Sect. II, 2.

[20] In agriculture, the practical application of scientific results dates back to the beginning of the nineteenth century.

the relatively small increase in output per worker brought about by the "horizontal" specialization of the medieval artisan (blacksmith, swordsmith, etc.). Most difficult to classify is *thirdly* the invention of machines which either create a novel product (like printing), or displace workers in the production of old products.

The first and the third phenomena appear as early as the Middle Ages, but do not, in our opinion, justify the labeling of the years from 1300-1600 A.D. as *early industrial capitalism:* the first phenomenon is visible in the textile industry of Florence, Flanders and other places (spinning, dying, weaving, etc., all in different enterprises), the third phenomenon appears, at the latest, about 1450 A.D. in mining; here belong also the invention of the compass, of gunpowder and the improvement of the art of sailing. We are unable, however, to consider the type of vertical division of labor as, e.g., described in the first chapter of Adam Smith's *Wealth of Nations* as a mere *continuation* of the textile processes of Florence and Flanders, primarily because they represented only a small extension and reorganization of millennia-old production processes, and therefore failed for many hundred years to stimulate a development outside their particular field; as in printing there is, so to speak, inbred in the production process a certain temporal order which leads also to the distribution of the various functions to various workers, but there was no insight that by an *artificial* break-up of the production process great increases of output per worker or man-hour could be obtained. Likewise machinery making its appearance before 1600 appeared primarily where without it no production at all would have been able—as an overcoming of natural obstacles rather than as saving in manpower. Introduction of machinery for the latter aim is visible only in the second half of the seventeenth century.

If we take the systematic introduction of either the

first or third process as criterion, then it seems impossible to date before 1600 A.D.[21] the age of industrial capitalism, in the sense of a continuous transformation of production processes.

To the best of our knowledge the only *systematic* attempts to explain the revolutionary transformation were brought forward by the German economist and sociologist Max Weber;[22] we must refrain in this essay from discussing the *obiter dicta* which anybody writing about the period in question (whether economist, sociologist, historian, or theologian) could not resist enunciating. In a famous article, *The Protestant Ethic and the Spirit of Capitalism* (first published 1904/5, translated 1948, then republished with important additions in his *Collected Papers on the Sociology of Religion*), and in an important supplement (not translated) *The Protestant Sects and the Spirit of Capitalism* (reprinted in the *Collected Papers*), Weber stresses the assistance which the "capitalist spirit" (meaning the spirit of *industrial* capitalism) experienced from the new religious developments especially from Calvinism. He did not maintain that the phenomenon, "industrial capitalism", could be explained exclusively from the rise of a new spirit.[23]

[21] The reader may study the large material collection in W. Sombart, *Modern Capitalism* II, Ch. 45. Unfortunately Sombart at no place arranges his material chronologically, though, thanks to his careful documentation, the reader is enabled to do so. Sombart's distinction between manufacture and factory is not generally accepted.

[22] The spotlight which Sombart has thrown in special studies on the influence of war and of luxury on "capitalism" has never been very revealing for this writer. Ancient luxury has scarcely ever been surpassed; and, as to war, it should be noted that the armies of later Roman times numerically exceeded by far those of the seventeenth century, when 25,000 men were considered an unusually large army and Gustav Adolph undertook the conquest of Germany and Austria with only 13,000 men.

[23] A full understanding of Weber's position can be obtained only by studying the pertinent parts of his giant work, *Economy and Sociology* (especially "The City", Part II, Ch. VIII), the exten-

In his *Lectures on Economic History* (see footnote 23), he put into the foreground the existence of the *free worker,* which enforced a rational organization of production. Let us turn first to this factor.

Weber's opinion is clear: in an economy in which all production is tightly controlled in a guild organization as in China—an organization inimical to novelties—new methods of production cannot originate. Ancient economy, indeed, did not have such a tight guild organization, but the free craftsman who survived was not needed by the employers who always could use slaves; the craftsman remained craftsman. In the West, on the other hand, the free status of the city dweller, in contrast to the status of the peasant as bondsman, if not serf, created a migration from the rural area to the town—never the other way round—and hence an excess population of craftsmen, which no work-parcelling policy of the guilds could keep at a tolerable standard of living. Some of the craftsmen were able to rise to the status of entrepreneurs, especially in industries producing new products, the less able or less fortunate members were proletarized and created the new stratum of free workers, which was either unknown or unimportant in ancient times.

Industrial capitalism and religion. Weber started with the never-disputed, nor elsewhere-explained, fact of the economic superiority of the Protestant parts of Germany over the Catholic parts. He could have referred to many similar facts, e.g., the well-known economic loss which France, flourishing under the régime of Colbert till 1675, suffered from the expulsion of the Huguenots a dozen years later and the economic gain of the countries which

---

sive and very impressive studies on the *Economic Ethic of the World Religions* (now in the three volumes of the *Collected Papers* mentioned above, translated 1950, 1952, 1958) and the *Lectures on General Economic History* (translated by F. H. Knight, 1950).

received them.[24] The very strong influence of religious rules on civilization, and its economic aspects, becomes particularly clear in Weber's studies on the *Economic Ethic of the World Religions,* mentioned in footnote 23; only the hardened dogmatist can resist Weber's arguments after having studied them. In addition, the reader may consult for the eighteenth century and the beginning of the nineteenth descriptions of the difference in the style of life of, say, the French settlers in Louisiana and their Anglo-Saxon neighbors.[25]

The Capitalist Spirit. The discussion has been confused by Weber's unfortunate habit of laying particular stress on the *ethical motives,* and turning to differences in behavior only in some parts of his famous first article. He considers, e.g., the German merchant prince, J. Fugger (sixteenth century) as medieval, because his statement —I want to make profit as long as I can—lacks the ethical tinge characteristic for later Puritans, who had the same aim of amassing unlimited wealth. Clearly if no differences in economic behavior could be found—differences which were not mentioned at this point by Weber—the economic result could not be different. What do we find? a) The "calling" (vocation) of a Calvinist was "an invitation to live the orderly and settled life ordained for one by God, and to perform all the duties pertaining to it." This is

[24] It has been pointed out that in the host countries of the Huguenots, success was not due to their faith but to their position as "aliens". But this interpretation does not explain the economic decay of France, which is admitted by a critic of Weber: H. Sée, *Economic History of France* (in German, 1930) vol. I, pp. 374-377. Nor would it explain the disproportionate role which the Huguenots play today in the economic life of France; and of course not the economic situation in Germany referred to in the text.

[25] We refer here to the novels of Charles Sealsfield: *Sketches of Life in the Western Hemisphere.* The author was an Austrian ex-monk who travelled in the eighteen-twenties in the Southern states of the U.S.A.

a quotation from the sharpest critic of Weber, H. M. Robertson (*Aspects of Economic Individualism,* 1933, p. 70 of the 1959 edition). Robertson maintains that in the early times of Calvinism, and of course with Luther and Calvin, it was primarily industry and not covetousness which was encouraged by the Protestant doctrine. Be that as it may, this attitude, like the related desire to prove by some worldly success that one belonged to the "Lord's Elect," [26] would greatly increase the number of "capitalists," in the sense of people whose income was large enough to save some amount and for whom moderation in consumption was a religious command. Similar preachings of Catholic clerics (and even Lutheran pastors) would not have the same effect, because in these religions salvation did not depend on the style of life and the concept of the "Lord's Elect" was unknown. Here salvation depended on fulfilling a ritual, on repentance or on the belief in the ever-present saviour, Jesus Christ.

b) The additional amount of capital was available primarily to members of the same church, or sect, who had proved their reliability by their way of life, regardless of their social origin. At least in countries where the guild system was not fully developed, or the ingenuity of man could be concentrated on novel products (those who were not guild controlled), especially in England [27] and the

[26] According to Calvin, original sin damned mankind to hell, excepting those people whom the Lord elected at birth to be forgiven and to be raised to heaven. The question whether he belonged to the Lord's Elect greatly worried Cromwell on his deathbed.

[27] It has been pointed out that the Church of England—the country which is usually considered the cradle of industrial capitalism—was not Calvinistic. This argument overlooks the fact that after the return of the Stuarts, the bulk of the Presbyterians and Independents were forced by political legislation, which deprived the dissenter of his voting rights, to return to the mother church, where historians take note of them under the heading of "Low Church." The opposition between Church and Chapel has not yet fully vanished.

Netherlands, a select group (primarily former craftsmen) were enabled to remodel, step by step, the methods of production.

c) Not all fields of activity were open to them. The monopoly-usury[28] capitalism of the late Middle Ages, in which the Fuggers made and lost their fortune, was precluded on religious grounds. Commercial activities were of course not precluded, but restricted by the large monopolies which controlled the trade with India and Latin America.

The spirit of the times indulged in fantastic projects, possibly as a counterpoint of the adventurous gains expected from the discovery of new continents; if taken up by the experienced, non-gambling group of adherents of the new religion who alone could command financial help from their co-religionists, a systematic attack on antiquated methods of production would result. This attack would not only spread around the older ideas of vertical division labor, but sooner or later realize the long-sought workable steam engine, until in the nineteenth century the scientific discoveries in electricity and chemistry were applied in practice by the new type of entrepreneur, whose origin now was not limited to a specific religious group. The contribution of a less fantastic and more rationalistic attitude of the times to the big transformation is not to be denied; but by itself it did not suffice as is shown by the economic development of rationalistic France even in the era of enlightenment.

The era of "amassing unlimited wealth" is not the seventeenth century but the nineteenth; we refrain from try-

[28] The term "usury" is here used in the modern sense. In the Middle Ages and in the time of the Reformation it encompasses *any* charge of interest. But the original Christian prohibition of interest was long before the Reformation qualified by the permission of charging interest for productive loans, where the interest represented a share in the borrowers' profit from the invested capital.

ing to estimate the share of Calvinism in this period; it was surely smaller than in the preceding periods, despite the changes in Calvinism which had occurred. Industrial capitalism is in full swing when the nineteenth century starts; what transformed commercial capitalism is no longer the question.

Other historical-institutional factors. We return to the seventeenth and eighteenth centuries, the centuries of the transformation. Two important phenomena have been neglected.

We must first consider a peculiar tendency of commercial capitalism to erect a barrier to industrial capitalism, the essence of which is *mass production.* Apart from the trade in necessities during the late Middle Ages (wool, grain and textiles, all transported by waterways), the caravan trade of old and the trade in commercial capitalism were, crudely speaking, 1000 per cent-profit-margin trade. In general, however, the turnover was small (a point stressed so much by Sombart), and the bulk of the people living from trade had an income no larger than that of the average craftsman; however, there were a few who, knowing how to increase the volume of the trade, became very rich. In other words, trade had a strong gambling element, which made it attractive compared with industrial production (the craftsman never got rich),[29] and left little energy for the improvement of the methods of production. This state of affairs lasted, to some extent, well into the eighteenth century, when a considerable

[29] W. Sombart, *Modern Capitalism,* Part I, Ch. 39, collected the material about mark-ups in the late medieval trade (under the misleading title: "How wealth was obtained in the artisan's economy," because he refuses throughout to treat the Middle Ages trade on a basis different from crafts). He concludes: "Indeed, merchandise was traded in the middle ages with a considerable mark-up. A similar computation of the mark-up in the production is impossible."

part of the wealth of Holland and England was traders' wealth. But it is precisely this type of semi-gambling profit which ran counter to the spirit of Protestantism and, for some time, shifted the centers of improved industrial production into Protestant regions. In the nineteenth century, commercial trade lost its gambling aspects, and mass turnover with small profit per unit became the rule, with few exceptions, in trade as well.

Secondly, we want to point to an indirect consequence of the age of exploration and the occupation of large parts of America and Asia by European countries. True, the products amassed there and put at the disposal of Europe were either new luxury goods (especially spices, tobacco, sugar) or precious metals. These were additions to European consumption and were not able to set free resources either in Europe or elsewhere for investment proper, that is, the erection or expansion of plant and equipment. But the trend to falling wages, probably caused by the rise of population, and the price inflation, caused by the exploitation of the silver mines and gold deposits in America in the second half of the sixteenth century, could not fail to increase greatly the profit margin in manufacturing, making investment in this sector much more attractive than in the Middle Ages.[30] The objection has been raised that it

[30] Our result is obtained from the standard work of G. Wiebe, *Zur Geschichte der Preisrevolution des 16. und 17.* Jahrhunderts (1895) esp. pp. 125-131. Those later studies which we were able to consult confirm Wiebe. E. J. Hamilton, *American Treasure and the Price Revolution in Spain 1501-1650* (1934) is difficult to use in the present context, because Spain had in that period a kind of copper standard, the price index for silver in terms of the copper currency doubling from 1550 to 1600. It is, however, hard to avoid the conclusion that in Spain wages increased more than the prices of agricultural products (for which alone material is available), probably because of the great manpower demand of the Spanish army. If this conclusion is correct, then an important stimulus to industrialization was absent in Spain. (A similar development can be observed in Belgium; we refer to the work of Verlinden and others.) Of W. Beveridge, *Prices and Wages in England,* only one

was primarily agricultural products which rose in price, not manufactures. This is exaggerated: goods like iron, building materials, shoes, and cloth also rose substantially in price. Furthermore, for novel goods neither price comparisons nor cost-price comparisons are possible.[31]

Summarizing the preceding discussion, we find:

1) Industrial capitalism required a larger current capital flow than the period of commercial capitalism: this was provided by the religiously motivated consumption restriction of Calvinism and the related sects and by the preference which co-religionists because of their orderly life enjoyed as borrowers.

2) It required entrepreneurs interested in the improvement of the methods of production: the exclusion of usury capitalism, the limitations to commercial capitalism, the spreading of a rationalistic spirit generated the new type.

3) It required absence of central imperial control and legal protection, both existing only in the West as heritage of the feudal period.

4) It required relatively large profit per unit of output to stimulate the competition of investment in production with investment in trade; the price inflation of 1550-1650 provided this opportunity. That this opportunity was used in the way described (in contrast, e.g., to the inflation under Diocletian) was due to the phenomena described under 2 and 3.

---

volume has been published (1939). The price of cloth more than doubled from 1550 to 1601 (p. 87).

[31] A regular flow of capital funds cannot be converted into real investment without the assistance of banks, exceptional cases being granted. By themselves, however, banks cannot create real capital, except by a process called "forced saving" by the economists, always of small significance and virtually absent before the eighteenth century. The banks' original function was to prevent a deflationary pressure from materializing, by collecting and lending funds that otherwise would be hoarded.

5) In addition it required cheap labor, which was provided by the overcrowding of the crafts since at least 1500 A.D.

All these factors were necessary conditions, and certainly they appeared on the scene only once in the history of mankind.

4

THE RISE OF EXPERIMENTAL SCIENCE

A) The meaning of experimental science

We are now concerned with the question of why experimental science arose only in the Western world, aside from some beginnings in the school of Alexandria. It began about 1600 with Galileo in the field of physics, and somewhat later in chemistry with Boyle, though one might postpone the beginning of scientific chemistry to Lavoisier, 150 years later, as the first chemist who insisted on rigorous quantification. We must stress that experimental science does not mean simply making experiments. It consists in integrating the results of experiments into a theory, law or model which explains past events and predicts future events, provided that the conditions under which the experiments were undertaken were or will be satisfied. This proviso is usually not fulfilled, except where artificial isolation is possible, a point to which we shall return. Hence, to obtain an explanation or prediction of all essential features of a past or future event, it is necessary to modify any general theory by special theories or by practical knowledge.

The phrase, "integrating the experiments into theory," is the core of our definition. It means that the cause-effect relationship established in an experiment is interpreted as proof of a general law, very frequently by reference to other experimental results or to laws already established.[32] Thus we measure for various distances the time needed by a falling body to reach the surface of the earth from the moment at which the fall began; then we formulate the law apparently governing the fall: distance of the fall equals the square of time passed multiplied by a constant characteristic for the earth. And the logic of the argument which performs this integration and formulates a new law is almost always so complicated that the help of the symbolical calculus called mathematics is required, not only to avoid logical errors but to discover in the available material relationships which the most powerful human mind would have been unable to find without the help of mathematics; e.g., mathematics allows us to deduce the law of falling bodies from the more general law of gravitation.

B) *Pseudosociological explanations*[33]

The absence of experimental science in ancient times has been attributed to social factors, usually by scholars who followed a fashion or a dogma and ignored the historical facts. There were, indeed, social factors, and we shall discuss them at the end of this section.

Here some quotation of what we consider the wrong approach must suffice: "This mischievous separation of

[32] Koyré (*op. cit.*) concludes his paper on Galileo and Plato with the statement that in scientific experimentation "the formulation of the postulates and the deduction of their implications antecedes and guides the recourse to observation." He evidently considered it unnecessary to spell out what is implied in his formulation, viz., that observation may force a modification of the original "postulates," nor the particular role of mathematics, which he stressed so often in his basic studies on Galileo.

[33] We must limit ourselves to a few examples. Other cases are mentioned, critically, in Koyré, "The Significance of the Newtonian Synthesis," in *Journal of General Education* (July 1950) especially footnote 6.

the logic from the practice of science [meaning technical activity] was a result of the ancient cleavage of society into freeman and slave."[34] There was no relation between modern science and modern technology in the first two centuries of the former. It is also asserted that it was the abolition of slavery and the substitution of free craftsmen which made modern science possible.[35] But slavery had vanished in Europe by 500 A.D. at the latest, and it is hard to see how such a development could have caused a basic intellectual change more than a thousand years later. Even Needham, whose authority for China we shall have to invoke later, states: "Part of the story undoubtedly concerns the social changes in Europe which made the association of gentlemen with the techniques respectable."[36] How does he know that Archimedes or the Alexandrian school did not enlist the help of craftsmen? Moreover, the social separation alluded to was one of the main characteristics of the eighteenth century, especially in England, and was certainly not applicable to Athens, socially the most egalitarian country that ever existed, except for the existence of slavery.

It is not realized that the human mind, when dissatisfied with a purely magical explanation of events in nature, will turn first to the relatively simple nonmagical explanation called "speculation."

C) *Speculation*

The essential difference between the nonmagical approach of speculation and the approach of modern science is

[34] B. Farrington, *Greek Science*, p. 303 (1944-1951).

[35] The same, quoted by Des Noettes, in *Le Mercure de France* (May 1932).

[36] J. Needham, *Science and Civilization in China*, vol. III, p. 155.

that speculation yields a type of explanation of observable phenomena that is not testable and never allows prediction. The overwhelming attraction of speculation for the human mind has three causes. First, it cannot be refuted by experience, in contrast to the statements of modern science. Second, it requires a type of ingenuity in thinking possessed only by great minds—productive however, of definite results within a *few years* of mental concentration, as contrasted with the centuries of experimentation and other observations required by the approach of modern science. Third, it can be cast into language analogous to the daily experience of human beings and is therefore, in a sense, intelligible to the average human mind.

Some brief remarks are in order concerning the principle of experience as the ultimate test of the validity of a theory of real events, especially since untestability and unpredictability are clearly drawbacks, which will also have to be discussed in the proper place. Here we note that the principle mentioned is of modern origin. The best proof is the surprise enunciated by most laymen and many historians of science about the great ancient astronomers' rejection of the heliocentric hypothesis of Aristarchus. They could not accept it, because this hypothesis implied that the positions of the stars in winter would appear shifted from their position in summer, and such a shift was not observable. In fact, it was not observed before the beginning of the nineteenth century.[37]

Returning to the third point, are not ideas like the following easily understandable? "Every origination must be considered as a combination and every destruction as a separation of the four imperishable elements: earth, air,

[37] Copernicus' explanation of this phenomenon (from the enormous distance of the stars) could have been given also in ancient times—one of the numerous scientific examples of the difficulty of using apparently unrelated observations in theory formation.

fire and water."[38] Another example is the brief formulation of atomism: there is nothing but atoms and the void. We grant that there have been speculative systems, like that of Heraclitus, which were not easily understandable, but their influence was negligible.[39]

After our statement at the beginning of this chapter about the nature of experimental science, we trust that the mere presence of an experiment in the speculative age will not be cited as argument against our position. The acoustic experiments of the Pythagoreans were famous, but the school was destroyed. Speculative philosophers like Anaxagoras and Empedocles demonstrated the corporeality of the air by experiment; but it is characteristic that they stopped when they had proved what was needed, together with material from practical knowledge, in their speculative systems. Aristotle is said to have possessed a laboratory, but where in his teaching is there a proposition which could be said to have an experimental basis?[40] And yet the question whether heavy bodies fall faster than less heavy bodies did not need a Leaning Tower of Pisa to be decided by experiment.

The fact that speculative systems are based on analogies and not on tests has a natural drawback. It creates a multiplicity of systems. Still, if it were not for Aristotle's interest in history of doctrine, we would not know much about ancient speculation aside from Plato and Aristotle.

We can omit Plato here, for he was not much con-

[38] Empedocles, see, e.g., W. Windelband, *History of Ancient Philosophy* (English translation), pp. 73-74.

[39] The seductive power of speculation is most remarkable in the work of Galileo, whose last publication on comets is purely speculative, and who considered as unnecessary simple experiments which would have demonstrated the validity of what today is called the Galilean principle of relativity.

[40] According to A. P. Usher, *A History of Mechanics* (rev. ed. 1954), p. 87, Aristotle's analysis of mechanics and his formulation of the laws of motion are very closely associated with his metaphysical doctrines.

cerned with the way the real world mirrored the world of ideas, except for the fact that it rarely did so faithfully. The great superiority of the Aristotelian system, which impressed first the Arabs and then the thinkers of the West from 1100 to 1500 and even later, has been based primarily on three characteristics (apart from refuting such unacceptable doctrine as the Eleatic doctrine of the impossibility of motion). First, it takes as a starting point what every human being experiences: the entelechy of the living substance, the easily understandable distinction between form and matter; as far as we know, Aristotle was the first to present in systematic order the functions of the human mind: perception, associated with the power of distinction and a minimum of judgment, then memory (both qualities possessed by at least some animals)—functions that allow man to build up a stock of experience, and to proceed to productive activity (τεχυη) and rational consideration.[40a] Second, it organizes not only the world around us, but also our thinking, in the logic. Third, it rounds off the metaphysical knowledge of the nature of being and the structural analysis of thinking by a vast empirical collection of what was known about the world around us, satisfying the human curiosity about nature, as, a century before, Herodotus had satisfied the curiosity about history.

The criticism of details which occurred even in ancient times, and the cry for independent empirical research, seldom implemented except in astronomy, could make no headway against such a gigantic intellectual achievement for more than 1700 years. There is only one point

[40a] These ideas are scattered over various writings of Aristotle. The arrangement above is taken from C. Prantl, *Geschichte der Logik im Abendland* (1855) vol. 1, p. 106. Characteristically, Aristotle continues the arrangement into the realm of metaphysical speculation. The common root of these activities, the νομσ, is supposed to grasp on the one hand the transcendental-divine, on the other hand the multiplicity of the individual.

on which Aristotle was not victorious: he could not prevent the application of mathematics in astronomy. That his empirical knowledge was only descriptive could not be considered a defect in times which did not know of an explanatory science predicting the events of nature. When we turn to the rise of experimental science around 1600 A.D., we shall come back briefly to Aristotle. At this point it is necessary to clarify the position of the school of Alexandria in our analysis of Greek science.[41]

D) *Alexandria*

Concurrent with the rise of speculation, one science in the modern sense was developed—mathematics—because it is rooted in the same attitude of mind, namely, contemplation. It found application in the real world, not in connection with experiments but in its relation to the equally old science of astronomy, the science of the regularities in the movements of the heavenly bodies. Prediction based on such regularities does not require the cru-

[41] It has been maintained that the school of Aristotle produced at least one great experimenter, Strato. And indeed the reader is impressed with the description of an experiment of Strato's mentioned in Farrington, *op. cit.*, pp. 174-176. A closer study of Strato's system, however, as presented, for example, in E. Zeller's famous *Philosophie der Griechen,* Part II, Sect. 2, 3rd German edition, pp. 901-910, clearly shows that this experiment was imbedded in a large speculative treatise and that Strato's procedure in general does not at all resemble the modern experimental method.

What we refer to here as speculation persists, of course, as imagination or, as Mach calls it, "instinctive knowledge" in the creative work of modern science. As a famous example we may mention the fact that Hertz's experiments concerning radio waves originated in a term in Maxwell's formulae introduced on the basis of a hunch and without any good experimental reason. The difference from speculation proper is that the imaginative anticipations in modern science are not considered part of the adopted body of science until confirmed by tests.

cial clause of experimental science—"other things being equal."

This type of science was not limited to astronomy. In medicine it is known, and still plays a great role, as the clinical method. It could be applied here with relatively great success because of the far-reaching isolation of the human organisms from their surroundings, and the vast number of very similar organisms and observations of regularities. But the desire of the human mind to obtain a generally applicable *explanation* of observations was so great that in medicine this strict clinical method, allegedly introduced by Hippocrates, was rapidly replaced by speculative theories. The most important was that of Galen, whose bloodletting prescriptions were probably responsible for the death of hundreds of thousands of people, among them Washington and Byron.

The extension of the method under consideration to other fields met unusual difficulties and was not successful, except, to some degree, in meteorology, until scientific statistical methods were developed in the last hundred years.

As is well known, the development of mathematics in Greece coincided with that of nonmagical speculation. For centuries, important contributions to mathematics were made all over the Hellenic world. Why, at the end of the fourth century A.D., were the mathematical-astronomical activities limited almost exclusively to Alexandria, while philosophy became ethics and eventually a new religion? We do not claim to have an answer that is completely satisfactory though we shall later allow ourselves some surmises. Here we shall take this fact of concentration in Alexandria as a starting point for examining the problem of the absence of an experimental science in the ancient world.

E) From Alexandria to the seventeenth century

Our first point, indeed a social factor, will appear ridiculously crude to most readers. We hasten, therefore, to add that, just before finishing this manuscript, we found that it had been mentioned before.[42] It is the absence of the art of printing and the lack of regular communication of results except by personal correspondence or at best by copying of manuscripts. A few illustrations may clarify the significance of this point. There must have been hundreds of mathematicians in the seventeenth century who were familiar with Fermat's tangent method for finding the turning points of functions, but only Newton and Leibniz developed the calculus. How then can we be surprised that Archimedes' basic insights into the calculus of integration, which can have been known only to a small circle, were not further developed? Or, to take an example from physics, thousands of physicists must have learned of the Michelson-Morley experiment, which contradicted both Copernicus-Kepler and Faraday-Maxwell's laws of electrodynamics, but seventeen years passed before one of them, Einstein, drew the logical conclusions of accepted physical theories and formulated the special theory of relativity.

Thus, the absence of printing greatly diminished the response to new ideas without which science in the modern sense cannot prosper, because a single man's or even a single school's capacities are limited. The school of Alexandria concentrated on mathematics and astronomy and, for the reason indicated, could not respond to the suggestions from Archimedes, who, although primarily a mathe-

[42] J. Mueller, "Ueber das Experiment in den physikalischen Studien der Griechen," *Naturwiss. Ver. zu Innsbruck,* XXIII (1896/7), quoted by Mach, *op. cit.*, p. 4.

matician, developed on an experimental basis what today in mechanics is called statics, as well as making contributions to some other important fields of physics. And so, with Archimedes, who apparently had no school, a great beginning died. It is only in a much later phase of the Alexandrian development that Heron and Ptolemy took up the work in experimental physics which Archimedes had begun many centuries before.[43] Why it ended is not clear; but if we recall the murder of Hypatia, the last known mathematician of this school, early in the fifth century A.D., we may surmise that in times of fanatical discussion of Christian doctrine the atmosphere for scientific research no longer prevailed in Alexandria.

Our analysis is still incomplete. None of the above discussion applies to China, where block printing was far older than Gutenberg, where no speculative system comparable to Aristotle's stifled scientific progress, and where the literary education for a career as an official could not conceivably have—and, in fact did not absorb—all the intellectual energies of so vast a civilization. Needham, the great scholar on whom we rely for our knowledge of Chinese development, remarked: "No contact was made between the great alchemist and the great mathematician."[44] Equating alchemist with physicist, let us take this brief statement as a starting point. There was a social-institutional element in the West, which does not seem to have had a counterpart in China, although it does not differentiate modern from ancient times. This is the institution of universities and the ensuing social position of the scholar, whether he was associated with a university or in bitter controversy with its professors. This position which the scholar in China, outside of the bureauc-

[43] Of course scientific work in the modern sense concentrated in Alexandria gradually: in the third century B.C. Archimedes, Aristarchus and Hipparchus in his early stage lived outside Alexandria.

[44] *Op. cit.*, vol. 3, p. 153.

racy, does not seem to have attained, extended from the jurist and theologian whose activities created Bologna, Paris, and Oxford, to any professor whose field was an acknowledged part of the humanistic tradition.

From ancient times, the quadrivium had held its place in higher education, and two of its parts were areas of mathematics. Even after the authority of Aristotle had been shaken by Renaissance philosophers, a professor of mathematics like Galileo, who dabbled in physics, had to disprove that great authority with the hard facts of experiment. Thus ancient civilization, while unable to create experimental science, indirectly made possible its rise in modern times through the legacies of Roman law and mathematics.[45] Belatedly it gave birth to a body of self-perpetuating, independent scholars. First a minority, then increasing in number, they were not to be silenced. With the double foundation of mathematics and experiment, the new science became unassailable, eventually vanquishing speculation, and forcing into the background any mere collection and classification of material.[45a]

[45] As is well known, Greek mathematics had been supplemented before Galileo by the further development of algebra during the Renaissance, and the acceptance of the decadic system, supposedly of Hindu origin. Since, in general, the influence of Greek mathematics on Hindu mathematics is established, we may be allowed to surmise that Hindu mathematicians knew Archimedes' tract on the "Sand-Reckoner," which contains the principles of the decadic system.

[45a] M. Weber, *Confucianism and Taoism,* Sect. VI (in: *Wirtschaftsethik der Weltreligionen,* 1920, vol. I, p. 437) finds the origin of the experimental component in modern science in the *art* of the Renaissance, particularly in the ambition of the typical artist to obtain eternal significance and social rank by raising art to science. Which science? The science the artists of this century knew was exclusively rationalistic. And did Michelangelo, Raphael, or whichever artist we may think of obtain social rank by becoming a scientist in any sense? Weber refers to the experiments which Leonardo made, and secondly to Zerlino's key-board experiments; do we know of any influence of these experiments on Galileo and his School? Weber, indeed, changes almost at once his approach: it was the economic and technical interests, especially

those of mining (!) which introduced the experiment into natural science. Any new method of production, of course has been preceded at *all times* by "experimentation." But this is not the same thing as saying that such experimentation generated *experimental science* which had not been the case in millennia. Weber concludes his comments by pointing to the pacification of the Chinese empire, which allegedly failed to suggest an improvement in the military use of gunpowder—as if not China at least since about 1000 A.D. had been subjected to barbarian cavalry invasions! The Mongolian and Manchurian invasions would have ended differently had the Chinese infantry known to fire like the Prussian infantry at Mollwitz or the British infantry at Minden.

5

MANNHEIM'S SOCIOLOGY OF HISTORICAL-IDEOLOGICAL KNOWLEDGE

In the complex world of higher civilization, man has to take a stand. At least he has the opportunity to make statements on subjects outside his professional sphere. These statements frequently take the form of general propositions, claiming to explain what is happening, or proposing what is to be done; but rarely do they satisfy any scientific criteria, as they have been developed since Aristotle. We shall discuss these criteria later. At this point, we merely ask the reader to acknowledge that daily conversation does not make use of syllogisms, mathematical reasoning, scientific theorizing on the basis of experiments, or statistical analysis, and usually does not even bother to clarify its concepts. While it would be pedantic to ask for the application of the scientific method in every instance, and while short cuts are admittedly justified in many cases, the failure to acknowledge such procedure as required in principle makes the bulk of daily talk unconvincing and excludes it from knowledge proper.

In our opinion, this verdict has to be extended to cover not only most of the pseudoscientific publications in politics (some of which Mannheim analyzed in the essay, "Conservative Thought"), but also a very large part of the so-called explanations of events offered by historians. The conservative publications discussed by Mannheim were clearly an attempt to justify from "general principles," mostly formulated *ad hoc,* the particular political program of a group, which in turn reflected its interest or *social existence.* This is the core of Mannheim's "sociology of knowledge." As he points out, these publications aimed to rebut the equally ill-formulated and badly-argued "rationalistic" or "liberal" doctrines of the time, themselves nothing but an amplification of the slogans of the French Revolution. But shall we really write a sociology of knowledge around such statements as that of Adam Mueller, quoted by Mannheim,[46] that possessions are "extensions of the limbs of the human body," or "feudalism is the amalgamation of person and thing"? An examination of this kind of literature would scarcely allow us to draw any conclusion for the serious investigations of social science.

Thus, in accord with tradition, we mean by ideology the nonscientific way in which certain groups formulate their programs of practical policy in the widest sense of the word, and the pseudoscientific or, at best, superficial theories whereby their advocates try to prove the superiority of such programs, and on the basis of which, many, if not most, claim to explain events. This concept of ideology, which lays all stress on conceptual clarity, consistency, and method in the argument, seems at first glance to be at variance with Mannheim's concept of "total ideology," in both *Ideology and Utopia* and S.K. There the *total* structure of the mind of an epoch or group is under the indictment of being falsified by the inevitable perspective in which every member intellectually sees every intellectual problem. Actually Mannheim, who from the outset excluded natural science, soon started to modify his strictures further, first, by never including the great sociologists of his time (who frequently are quoted as authorities); then, by admitting even in *Ideology and Utopia*

[46] K. Mannheim, "Conservative Thought," reprinted in *Essays in the Sociology of Knowledge,* p. 105.

the possibility of a perspective-free political sociology; third, in certain reformulations in S.K.; and last in his posthumously published *Sociology of Mind.*[47]

One reason for the introduction of these modifications is obvious: there is no well-defined structure of mind characteristic of *every member* of the group. In a more elementary way, if we talk of the structure of mind of, say, the "bourgeois," we assume that it exists because of the overwhelming influence of human egotism on its behavior. Primitive and superficial as this social psychology undoubtedly is, to deny the limiting power of this instinct would be sheer hypocrisy. World religions like Christianity and Buddhism became acceptable to more than a small circle of disciples only after being thoroughly transformed. What, we may ask, is there left of the Sermon on the Mount in Christian theology, let alone in Christian practice?

But if Mannheim's doctrines, like the earlier ones of Marx and Engels, had their roots in these undesirable sociological facts, then it is equally clear that the convictions of the human being will not in all cases be determined by the convictions of the group in which he grew up. Might he not find better prospects for satisfying the egotistical thirst for wealth or power by joining the opposition? And are we absolutely sure that such notions did not play a role, at least subconsciously, in the mind of aristocrats like Pericles or Mirabeau who led the democratic opposition?

Moreover, even if for the moment we concede to human egotism the overwhelming influence which, with few exceptions, Marx, Engels and Mannheim ascribe to it, we are faced with the equally serious question of the individual's ability to decide what is advantageous for him and

[47] K. Mannheim, *Essays on the Sociology of Culture,* Part I (1956).

what is not? Ten thousand dollars are, other things being equal, more advantageous than one thousand dollars. But how did an inhabitant of a state north of the Mason-Dixon Line decide in 1861 that the Union was more advantageous for him than secession? Indeed, many abolitionists took the opposite view.

Mannheim was not satisfied with such elementary considerations. Let us consider briefly his attempts at reformulation. First the S.K. article! Mannheim neither agrees with those authors who deny any influence of the scholar's social position on the validity of his statement, nor with those who treat these statements as completely invalidated by the influence in question, but takes what he considers an intermediate view: the identification of the assertor's position "implies only the suspicion that this assertion might represent merely a partial view"; and "every complete and thorough sociological analysis of knowledge delimits, in content as well as in structure the view to be analyzed" (S.K., p. 255). A suspicion may be enough ground for a grand jury to indict, but a court wants *proof* —or, to abandon a doubtful analogy, criteria are necessary to gauge the influence of the assertors' social position. Furthermore, to replace "invalidate" with "delimit" does not indicate the "limit" nor does it enable us to restate the assertion within its true limits.

Even in the S.K. article, Mannheim seems to have realized the weakness of his original formulation, for there follows, immediately after the passages quoted, a shift in his position, which apparently has not been noticed by his critics. The "given social position" is now defined as "outlook and attitude conditioned by the *collective* purpose of a group." (Italics mine.) The group is not the group to which the assertor belongs by birth or education, but as Mannheim's paper on conservative thought clearly shows, the group whose interests the assertor chooses to defend.

There are good reasons for the shift. It is impossible to explain from the social position of Burke, Adam Mueller, and Stahl the context of their main propositions.[48] If one adds Burke's great adversary, the left-wing Whig, Charles Fox, son of one of the richest peers of England, Mannheim's original position threatens to become ridiculous. On the other hand, that the conservative ideology of the nineteenth century reflects the social position of the ruling group, and that the rationalism of the Enlightenment had at least one root in the opposition of the *roture* to the hereditary nobility, were well known before Mannheim.

Not much seems to have been gained by this reformulation. On the contrary, under the first formulation we would suspect anybody's statement which tallies with the perspective of the group to which he naturally belongs. Now we also must suspect statements made by authors who voluntarily left the natural group and became advocates of the opposition. Actually, we are forced to do so. Marx and Engels, regardless of their descent from a bourgeois group, were revolutionaries first and last. Their practical program and judgment, if not their scientific work, were certainly influenced by this fact. How else can we explain that they expected the collapse of capitalism whenever a financial crisis broke out, although the concentration of production in the hands of a few capitalists had surely not yet reached the degree stated in the first volume of *Das Kapital* as precondition? Furthermore, what induced Engels, who was experienced as was no other revolutionary in the management of business, to shy away from indicating the path which the communist

[48] F. Stahl, the theorist of Christian conservatism; E. von Simson, the moderate liberal who was twice chosen to offer the German Emperor's crown to Prussian kings and who was, at the time of his death, president of the highest German tribunal; and Karl Marx all shared social origin in the middle class and descent from Jewish ancestors.

economy would have to follow after the collapse of capitalism, and to devote himself instead to linguistic and military studies? These examples could be multiplied.

But let us return to our basic methodological question. One can understand that Mannheim, initially, was not satisfied with the willingness of his predecessors to grant exceptions to the rule that an author's opinions are influenced by his social position. Unless a rule could be found for the exception (we would say: in terms of probability), the concession made seemed to imply that any author's opinions are colored by his natural perspective, unless they are not. On the other hand, the historical-biographical facts disproved Mannheim's original radical proposition.

Before trying to formulate a more acceptable statement, let us briefly have a look at what Mannheim originally considered an adequate solution to the problem of achieving a perspective-free sociology. He referred to a particular group "the relatively socially unattached intelligentsia" who are able to acquire a detached perspective as precondition for a sociology of knowledge (S.K., p. 252). A description of the elements from which one would have to detach oneself is missing. In his posthumous study of the role of the intelligentsia, we learn that Mannheim, by adding the word "relatively," wanted to allude to the fact "that intellectuals do not react to given issues as cohesively as, for example, employees and workers do." Indeed if all intellectuals, hence all scholars, were to be considered socially unattached, whose sociology of knowledge had Mannheim written? Even the new formulation is open to objection, since it seems to divide the intellectuals into socially attached and socially unattached groups.

What is still missing is the basic insight: a member of the intelligentsia is, like many other human beings, frequently uncommitted when he makes statements concerning subjects in which he is an "expert," in the sense that he follows the scientific rules of procedure. In all other respects, the members of the intelligentsia, except a small minority (which may be larger, however, than in other groups), are in the same danger as mankind in general of being influenced by the ideology of the group to which they naturally or professionally belong—an ideology which briefly reflects the *social position*. Thus, as a cohesive social group the relatively uncommitted intelligentsia does not exist.

We now understand more clearly what Mannheim did in introducing this concept: he, so to speak, personalized a set of objective rules. As we shall see later, Mannheim, in a posthumous study, actually tried to formulate these rules—a remarkable achievement which anticipated Felix Kaufmann's unfortunately never-fulfilled postulate.[49] If Mannheim had continued this work, his approach and that of Kaufmann, whose methodological stress was always on the rules of procedure, would have eventually converged at a point, we sometimes imagine, not very distant from the approach of the present paper.

Unfortunately, we know of no short but comprehensive publication in the field of philosophy of science to which we can refer the reader; nor have the philosophers reached agreement on all questions essential to our approach. Therefore, the next four chapters of this essay are intended as a sketch of these essentials. We shall then be able to return to our paramount problem. We admit, in passing, that in the natural sciences, the methodological investigations of philosophers have not been proved necessary to progress. The systematic social sciences, on the other hand, and especially historiography, might have profited at times from greater clarity about the methods of research.

[49] Felix Kaufmann, *Methodology of the Social Sciences* (1944).

PART II

The procedural rules of nonexperimental science

6

UNDERSTANDING AND BEHAVIOR

A) The role of understanding

The approach not only of Western science but of all "knowledge" of the world, except for some types of speculation, is deterministic as to the structure of the universe. It is only for the process of acquiring knowledge of the deterministically conceived universe that we are forced to admit certain modifications. One of these—the unpredictable productivity of the human mind—was discussed in Part I, Chapter 2; others will make their appearance later.

There may be philosophies which preach "Indeterminism" in a much more general sense than is acceptable to us and therefore negate the possibility of science. We consider ourselves free to disregard them, as we disregard the philosophy of solipsism, in which the author tries to persuade the reader that he, the reader, does not exist.

Western science owes its triumph over magic to its unquestionable "success," a criterion accepted by mankind long before the rise of modern science, in the nonmagical parts of practical knowledge as well as in magic. The criterion is inapplicable only in religion proper, that is, in religions which have been purified of magic and have replaced it with the prayer: Not as I will but as Thou wilt.

Experimental science thus appears as a refined continuation of what was the main portion of nonmagical practical knowledge. The principal rule is that of "isolation":

the exclusion of any factor whose influence is not to be studied in the experiment,[50] This exclusion ensures the possibility of repeating the experiment and minimizing the error of the experimenter.

Turning now to nonexperimental observations and sciences, we can limit ourselves to the social sciences (neglecting, e.g., meteorology) as the more complicated ones. The most important complication is the existence of an irreducible unit called human being (in contrast to the theoretically endless series of molecule, atom, electron, etc.) concerning whose behavior social science is not allowed to form arbitrary hypotheses, because direct observation is possible.

A human society is conditioned by the possibility of communication between its members: to some extent, human beings understand each other as human beings. The degree of mutual ("interpretive") understanding, of course, differs, but it is never zero.

B) Understanding and behavior

The existence of understanding between human beings is not controversial. What is disputed is that understanding is needed or useful for the establishment of a social science. Indeed, the web of mental acts (emotions, reflections, etc.) which precede and accompany a particular human act, is so complicated that after a very short while even the acting person himself largely forgets them, and, at best, remembers only a "dominant set." In economic theory, even this dominant set is further simplified in two

[50] The difficulty of adequate isolation shows up for example in the fact that the result of a chemical analysis may depend on whether the experimenter is wearing gold-rimmed spectacles or not.

respects. First, explanation of the acts is considered the task of other branches of social science (sociology, social psychology, cultural and social anthropology), and only the decisions which lead to a specific economic action are taken into account. Second, not individuals but groups (a term to be discussed later) are considered, and deviations from a typical group behavior are considered to cancel out in both an over-all description and an explanation of economic reality. It is possible that this simplification has gone too far. But would it not appear that economics is based on observations of behavior and not on understanding? Moreover, since all science of reality must be built on observations, cannot this procedure be extended to the other social sciences, and cannot understanding (introspection) be completely eliminated? To clarify this point, we shall use an illustration from Robert MacIver's *Social Causation* wherein he compares a paper driven by the wind with a man fleeing from a pursuing crowd. "The paper knows no fear and the wind no hate, but without fear and hate the man would not fly nor the crowd pursue." [51] The first question is how the observer knows that what he sees is not, say, a race but a pursuit.[52] A good answer would be that a pursuit has behavioristic properties —for example, shouts of the crowd that a race would not have. But then it is behavior, not understanding, which gives the correct interpretation. In more general terms, do we not have the following dilemma: Either "inside" mental acts are uniquely correlated with observable behavior, in which case we can build social science on behavior; or they are not, in which case we have no way of ascertaining the mental act?

This dilemma is spurious, for we have silently included

[51] Robert MacIver, *Social Causation*, p. 299.

[52] Jules Verne, in *Six Weeks in a Balloon*, describes an adventure in which the heroes of the plot mistake a pursuit for a race.

in behavior understandable talk, which the extreme behaviorist would not admit. In positive terms:

1. Society is based on the willingness of the human being to acknowledge as other human beings entities which look similar and to ascribe to them similar mental experiences. As human beings, we reject the alternative interpretation of the observed process as analogous to a Brownian movement.[52a] Hence we interpret talk not as a sound as that of the rain, but as having a meaning. This attitude greatly influences man's actions; it is at the root of the definition of human action, but it does not exhaust the contribution of understanding.

2. Meaningful talk rarely reveals adequately the mental processes inside the talker. To supplement the talk, the observer draws, carefully and critically, on his own mental experience, which enables him to distinguish between what we called the all-embracing jumble of mental acts and the dominant set. Not only the careful scholar and the successful politician, but also the layman who well understands other people, can in this way amplify greatly his ability to interpret the slightest variation in behavior as indicator of a differentiation in motives, and their further consequences for human action. Communication from other human beings further enriches this experience. Thus the observer can fathom what an event A, never experienced by him, implies for the action of people affected by A; in other words, the observer can predict the change in behavior in consequence of A, though he himself has never experienced A. Few readers of "Macbeth" have gone through his experience, but most have no difficulty in understanding him.

3. The interpretation of the actions of other entities,

[52a] If particles of gold are dissolved and suspended in water, they are permanently bombarded by the water molecules (at temperatures above absolute zero), and remain in motion the speed and direction of which can be examined mathematically with the help of the probability calculus.

performed by beings similar to the observer, and the supplementation of this interpretation by the process described above under (1) has been "tested" over several hundred thousand years in the successful co-operation of human beings (where co-operation includes hostile acts). This went on despite the possibility of misunderstanding in the individual case, including misunderstanding in psychological experiments and the interviews conducted by psychologists or other scientists, especially in anthropological excursions. Mankind, as a group, has had a great opportunity to understand the meaning of statements. Meaning denotes here something unreal; it is, in particular, not uniquely associated with particular sounds, or symbols, which are physical events (realities)—and through which meaning is usually communicated. Nevertheless, though unreal, it may act in the consciousness of the individual, thus influencing real events.[53]

Extreme behaviorism, which denies consciousness as an indispensable element in actual human behavior and in the constitution of the human society, rejects empirical material, but only so long as the scholar sits at his desk and not in his daily life or the conduct of experiments, a contradiction which does not seem to trouble him.[54]

4. We do not deny that the process of understanding is

[53] As is well-known, the prevailing psychological schools explain this fact by the hypothesis of a psycho-physical parallelism, which we need not discuss here.

[54] The writer is aware that behaviorism has undergone far-reaching changes since the time of J. B. Watson, and its present position may not differ greatly from the view set down here. Watson himself (*Behavior,* 1914, p. 330) attributed to language only the function of substituting for bodily movements. If I understand him correctly, he identifies language with sound, and since consciousness is to be eliminated from psychology (p. 27) he would have had no room for meaning as a non-physical entity. G. H. Mead's development indicates clearly the difficulties of behaviorism if its concepts are subjected to a searching analysis. The present writer owes a better understanding of Mead to the thorough analysis in M. A. Natanson's doctor-dissertation on Mead (New School for Social Research, 1953).

not foolproof, even in the case of individuals with whom the observer has been intimately acquainted for a long time.[55] It is less dangerous if the object of observation is group behavior, because errors may cancel out. Very frequently, it is undertaken only retrospectively by the historian, who, knowing the outcome, reconstructs the motives, a kind of history-writing which is inevitable in biographies, but has little explanatory value in the absence of some means of testing, a point to which we will return in Part III.[56]

We differ, therefore, from the behaviorist who denies the role of understanding and the "existence" of unreal entities like meaning. But we differ equally from any school that considers understanding (interpretation) by itself a reliable scientific tool in social sciences. The cor-

[55] Before the Battle of Liegnitz, 1760, Frederick the Great stated: "If two opponents have made war on each other for several years they obtain of the opponent's style of thinking and acting a knowledge sufficient to divine what the other side could have in mind." This knowledge, though, was far from complete. In the following year, Frederick did not divine that the same Austrian general would try to take by storm the fortress of Schweidnitz as soon as Frederick had, for purposes of provisioning, withdrawn its cover.

[56] Our results differ in only one important point from the interpretation in Theodor Abel, "The Operation Called 'Verstehen'," *American Journal of Sociology* (1948), reprinted in Feigl-Bradbeck, *Readings in the Philosophy of Science* (1953). In particular we agree with his statement: "Thus, all assertions based *only* (italics mine) on the evidence of understandability can be viewed as a case of 'misplaced familiarity'" (p. 685). Abel concedes that understanding can be particularly helpful in setting hypotheses even though it cannot be used to test them. But he seems to underrate greatly this function, which constitutes human society. We thoroughly disagree with Abel's conclusion: "The operation of 'Verstehen' does not, however, add to our store of knowledge, because it consists of the application of knowledge already validated by a personal experience." The purely personal experience of a Casper Hauser gave him scarcely any knowledge. Knowledge is not obtained by what Abel calls "personal experience" in the sense of an individual's particular and subjective mental experience. Knowledge always requires testing, in the wide sense defined in this essay—testing of hypothetically formulated propositions.

rectness of the concept of human society has been "tested" in daily life to the full satisfaction of everybody not prejudiced by palpably untenable dogmas. But the correctness of particular interpretations of actions, as undertaken in social science, must be tested by the particular tools of the science; and in the later chapters we shall sketch the pertinent rules of procedure.

Understanding provides human beings with a certain amount of common experience or practical knowledge as to the responses of other human beings to a given action of one of them; this practical knowledge is highly developed, e.g., in first class politicians. It leads to the establishment of rules of conduct which make human existence more pleasant and more predictable; we mean, of course, rules of typical conduct, not ethical norms. Institutions are crystallized rules of conduct.

C) The use of understanding

The social scientist makes use of the practical knowledge of rules of conduct in two respects: (1) to develop a classifying scheme of possible human actions, group relations, etc. ("categorization"), as Weber did in the first part of *Economy and Society*, or, in a slightly different way, Parsons-Shils in *Towards a General Theory of Action;* and (2) to formulate laws explaining action. At this point we must stress that the two processes are not independent. While, of course, a number of terms used in daily life are so clear and so tightly connected with a particular concept that they will appear with unchanged meaning in any scientific analysis of the real world, there are a substantial number of such terms (words, symbols) which do not possess these qualities, and an equally substantial number of both terms and concepts created in the process of analysis; the last two groups require particular care in definition.

The creation of new concepts (and the change in meaning of terms already in use) is by no means arbitrary but always adapted to the needs of explanation which will be described later in greater detail. It is this process, not adequately described by the medieval labels of either "nominalism" nor "realism," which mystified Marx and Engels (and on occasion Mannheim), and induced the former to retain, in an entirely changed form, the "dialectical method," and to confuse the change in the meaning of a term and the creation of new concepts with "fluidity" of meaning. Neo-Kantianism has the indubitable merit to have overcome the medieval dichotomy by introducing the concept of "validity of propositions," admitting at the same time the never-ending task of a science of reality in reformulating the conceptual apparatus. For the formulation of laws, of course, more is required than a "categorization," based on "understanding" and practical knowledge. In subsequent chapters, we shall develop the concept of a "model," and describe the methods of establishing it tentatively. Even in the most favorable case, it will not prove completely adequate for prediction in the nonexperimental sciences.

7

ECONOMICS AS A SOCIAL SCIENCE

A) Basic questions

The task of economics is to explain and predict events that directly refer to the provision of goods and services for man. This definition is too wide in one respect. Explanation and prediction of government action relating to this provision is excluded from economics though not the economic effects of such action. Classical economics proceeded on the basis of the practical knowledge of the rules of conduct, and, of course, the pertinent laws of nature. The complexity of society in all but the most primitive tribes required so-called "idealizing" assumptions to both typical but unorganized responses of man (e.g., profit maximization) and institutions (e.g., the structure of the market). Moreover, the economist had to treat a considerable number of events as "exogenous" and not to be explained or to be predicted in his science. This included not only events in nature and in the sphere called politics (where only the effect and not the causes are a concern of the economist), but also basic changes in the attitude of human beings, the explanation and prediction of which were left to sociology in the broader sense or to "social psychology."

Since the language used in describing actions and institutions was that of daily life, it required a powerful mind to create an economic theory which had relevance to the explanation of economic reality. The situation was made worse by the fact that neither the idealizing assumptions nor the results were confirmed by tests. Admittedly, testing material was scarce, but the absence of testing was at least partly due to the lack of recognition of the necessity for testing, a lack which marred the discussion of later generations on method. Less powerful minds, feeding on the masters, and always in the majority, overshadowed the outstanding work of the masters and provoked the derisive comments and the ideology theory of Marx and Engels. It was, indeed, to be expected that in choosing the idealizing assumptions and in the unmethodical reasoning, the ideological influence of the "social situation" would play some role.

The great transformation of economic theory in the second half of the nineteenth century (Schools of Lausanne and Cambridge) improved the situation in only one respect: by the use of mathematics they greatly reduced the danger of fallacious reasoning, though not of wrong idealization, and were able to extend theory to cases inaccessible to the classics. But economics still lacked the possibility of testing the premises, and never reached the goal of analyzing an economic disequilibrium with the same rigor as the economic equilibrium. Only when statistical analysis in the widest sense of the phrase was introduced, was economics raised to the level of a full-fledged science. Before discussing this last step, some remarks about the meaning of "idealization" are in order.

Idealization in physics seems to be interpreted primarily as the establishment of relations under the simplifying and isolating conditions of the experiment. The experimenter hopes to use the established results for explanation and prediction in the real world by systematic investigation of the possible disturbances in separate experiments, the results of which will be eventually superimposed; but it would be erroneous to think that this program is always carried out and that the reputation of the natural sciences is based on its fulfillment.

At this point, it is necessary to point out a second, even more general, root of idealization—the application of any symbolical calculus, especially of mathematics, in the explanation of the real world. The radically idealized nature of the concepts and propositions of this calculus, to which nothing in the real world exactly corresponds, creates a gap between observations and calculus. No experiment can be simplified to such an extent that its components satisfy the requirements of the calculus completely, nor is precise measurement in the sense of the calculus possible. For this reason, Aristotle opposed, and a number of Neo-Aristotelian social scientists today oppose, the use of mathematics; they do not realize how widespread the use of mathematical concepts has always been in daily life, practical knowledge, and even speculation. Aristotle's rectilinear movement of physical bodies is a mathematical concept; we use mathematics if we instruct somebody to turn around and to go back in the direction "opposite to the one in which he came."

The explanation of the apparent paradox as expressed in the gap is simple. Scientists assume that the gap (hence any error arising from it) can be made as small as desired.[57] In nonexperimental sciences the solution is a little more complicated. We shall discuss this point in a later subsection. Here let us briefly point out some peculiarities of idealization in the social sciences.

[57] According to Koyré ("Galileo and Plato," pp. 419-427) such a pragmatic formulation would not have been satisfactory to Galileo, who, as a Platonist, considered the Platonic "reminiscence" of the permanently, a priori existing "ideas" (among which the mathematical entities play the principal role) both a necessary and a sufficient condition for the harmony of the real world and mathematical construction. The present writer is not a Platonist; and Aristotle might have asked how the most precise knowledge of the "ideas" would help in explaining the real world, which is admittedly a very inadequate reflection of the ideal world.

For the social scientist who cannot experiment, idealization refers first to what is to be explained, namely, not every detail of the social process but only its relevant aspects, where the relevance differs in different contexts. Idealization refers secondly to the selection of the determining forms of behavior (or features of the natural surroundings) as typical. This means that the great majority of members in a specified group are said to react most of the time in a certain way to specified events; the group's reaction is therefore far more predictable than that of the individual, though, as we shall see in the next subsection, deviations do occur. Briefly, idealization means here treating all consumers as if they acted at all times according to type.

A few examples must suffice. The most important idealization in the theory of industrial capitalism is certainly the assumption that the firm strives for maximization of profit. The exceptions, like the case in which a traditional level of profits is all that the firm aims at, are considered negligible for two reasons: (1) exceptional behavior is not "contagious"—if one firm neglects to maximize profit where possible, this attitude will not induce a similar attitude in other firms with which the "negligent" firm is trading; and (2) negligent firms are weeded out by the process of competition.

The consumers' decisions can be either related to the market (buying goods and selling his services) where the consumer typically is motivated by his own advantage, or to outside decisions which are not "contagious": almsgiving, for example, does not typically induce the recipient to give alms.

Idealization, in our sense, is not identical with Weber's "idealtype," which is a personalization of important aspects of human behavior in an era, and, in our opinion, an unnecessary complication. In the present context, idealization allows us to ascertain the *real* type prevailing either generally or in a specific era—provided, of course, that such typical behavior exists. Statistically, the real type is expressed as the "mode" or the most frequent value (again, if there is one and only one) of a frequency distribution.

B) The statistical method

If the social world typically showed simple regularities like those of the astronomical world, prediction at least would be possible without further analysis. In general, the social world does not show regularities without complicated statistical analysis. This analysis is nothing but the refined form of Mill's "induction." It was rejected by the Neo-Kantians in favor of the isolating experiment, largely because they did not know of any rule concerning the number of largely identical observations of relations or coincidences required to allow the observer to formulate a rule by induction. This question has been attacked by modern statistics with some success, but that does not mean that theory can be considered superfluous.

The aim of statistical analysis is to show that the observed event can be explained by the concatenation of a number of systematic variables which leave as residue only random deviations. If the analysis is successful, it will show that a great number of apparently different events can be explained by the same set of forces, which, however, always operate in the phase of development just reached, and therefore produce different results at different times. As pointed out above, the forces mentioned here are represented, in particular, by the reaction of human groups, for example, groups of consumers, producers, investors, etc., to events of economic relevance—in short, group behavior functions. A few comments and illustrations must suffice here to clarify the procedure.

On the basis of common experience, or practical knowledge, the forces are entered in a specific way into a model, which is an economic theory specified by particular behavior functions. On the basis of historical-statistical material, the forces (appearing as coefficients or, more generally, functions in the model) are measured and tested. If the tests come out satisfactorily, the past is explained and, under certain conditions, future relevant events may be predicted.

As illustration we do not choose a theory of classical or neo-classical vintage, because its static character would require further comments on its explanatory and predictive value. We begin with a simple dynamic model, which means that there are related observed magnitudes of the same economic variable in various time periods, say at $t-2, t-1, t, t+1$ . . . Our first illustration is $Y_t = cY_{t-1} + v(Y_{t-1} - Y_{t-2})$, where Y denotes aggregate income, and c and v certain economic forces, namely, the response of consumers to income earned and the investors to changes in income. Any such model is, in principle, testable in two ways.

(1) From observations of changes in income over time we can by statistical analysis derive best fitting values for c and v; if certain statistical criteria are satisfied, the model, including the idealizing hypotheses, is empirically confirmed; except for a "break in the structure" (a term to be explained later) the model can be used for prediction.

(2) The values of c and v can be estimated from direct observation of the behavior of the groups concerned,[58] and if the tests are satisfactory, the model again is considered

[58] The distinction between the two types of testing and the limitation of natural science to the first type is well brought out in F. S. C. Northrop, *The Logic of Sciences and the Humanities* (Meridian Book reprint, 1959, p. 108).

confirmed. The explanation is complete only if, in addition to the measured forces (c and v in our model) and the behavior functions, there are given so-called "initial conditions"; that is, in the case of a difference equation of second order, the values of the variable—here Y—in two periods, which, in principle, can be arbitrarily chosen, say, the values of Y_j and Y_k. The number of initial conditions required equals the number of possible solutions of the equation system, and from these possible solutions the given initial conditions select one solution as the only solution in harmony with the course of real events.

Obviously the model is oversimplified; this needs no discussion. Much more important is the fact that the model claims something which in natural science is claimed only in astronomy, if at all: to explain and predict the course of events from the "initial conditions," namely, the initial magnitudes of the unknown variable (here the level of Y at two initial periods of time), and from the forces at work, here the coefficients c and v. This is not achievable in practice. At best we could hope to develop such "astronomical" models, valid for a short period, to be followed by another model. However, this attempt might fail for lack of sufficient observations to estimate and test the models. As an alternative we consider the "meteorological" model. To predict, this model makes use of established relations (natural laws, group behavior functions) and *current observations* concerning the behavior of some groups for which reliable behavior functions cannot be found, but whose behavior will influence the development of the principal unknown variable (Y in our case), or unknowns, in the future; current observations allow us to treat the variable in question as if it were "exogenous" (but known) or a kind of initial condition. Assume, for example, that current investment decisions affect income but with a time lag; eliminate the second term on the right side in our illustration and write $Y_{t-1} - cY_t = D_t$, where

D_t denotes the currently observed investment decisions. "Meteorological" models, though of great help in prediction, obviously furnish only an incomplete explanation of the past, a point to which we shall return in Part III.

In the applications of statistics, it is not as easy as in the experimental sciences to satisfy one essential condition—that is, clarity: to establish a one-to-one correspondence between symbols and language terms and, in particular, between language terms and economic events. A great number of erroneous "theories" and conclusions have originated in the investigator's silent assumption that this correspondence can be taken for granted.

We shall discuss later the difficulties encountered by modern economics in observing the procedural rules. But we may stress here the fact that, however great the difficulties are, their existence does not enhance the value of untested armchair theorizing; the latter is indispensable for tentatively establishing a model, which, however, without any assurance about the empirical validity of the idealizing assumptions, would be useless for both explanation of the past or prediction of the future.

C) Structure and causation in Mannheim

Before discussing the defects of the method described and its generalization for all aspects of social life, it seems worthwhile to compare our results with what Mannheim called in the posthumous *Essays on the Sociology of Culture* the "explanatory" and the "expository" procedure, and the "Structure of Events" and the "Causal Account,"[59] always remembering that what we have before us are not definite formulations but a draft, probably meant to be

[59] Mannheim, *Essays on the Sociology of Culture,* Part I, Sect. III, especially subsections 6-12.

thoroughly revised. The ultimate aim of a "sociology of mind," Mannheim states, must be to "interpret" the occurrence of an event by "detecting" its functions in the "equilibrium of the whole system" (or "structure"). The term "equilibrium" must not here be understood as referring to a lasting state of the system—the system being at rest except for exogenous intrusions. The stress is on *structure*,[60] meaning the constellation of forces: "a given structure depends on specific causation agents, and their absence may bring about the decay or modification of these structures." The causation agents are our behavior functions.

Mannheim's construction, therefore, foreshadows our present approach whose methodological peculiarities were, at the time he wrote, known only to few economists. Missing in his formulation are two elements: (1) that systematic social science can use only group behavior as causation agents; (2) the possibility of a "break" in the structure. There is, indeed, at one place a kind of mental reservation, which, however, has no systematic place in his new methodology: "To ignore the role of leadership and to deny the catalytic function of a single person is a distortion of the sociological interest." We shall return to this question later.

D) *Defects of the statistical analysis*

It must be conceded that the success of the procedure outlined here has been much smaller than that of the experimental sciences, partly because prediction in the ex-

[60] See, for example, *Ibid.*, p. 81: "It is this distinct aspect of actions which permits us to construe them as part of an equilibrium"; obviously "equilibrium" means here what we call "structure."

perimental sciences has a double meaning: prediction proper (like that of an eclipse, or, less successfully, of the weather or, rarely attempted, the appearance of comets) and technological prediction. The latter occurs whenever we can actually imitate to a sufficient extent the isolating features characteristic for the experiment. Thus we can predict that a bridge built according to the laws of physics will not collapse, provided there is observance of the rule that vehicles weighing more than ten tons are prohibited, and provided that maintenance rules are also observed. On the other hand, the predictions proper in meteorology have not been greatly superior to those of economics, at least until recently.

Economics participates in the glory gained for the majority of the natural sciences by the experimental method and technological prediction because of the philosophical attitude of Western civilization; namely, that all events are fully determined by natural causes, where the word "natural" now includes man and his actions. Let us admit that this is not fully justified because of certain inevitable drawbacks in the statistical method.

1. The method is applicable only where there is a typical group behavior, in statistical terms, where there is one and only one "mode" around which the observations (or relations) are grouped in such a way that the mean-square deviation is relatively small.

2. It is frequently impossible to find or observe all the systematic factors that caused the observed change in the dependent variable; hence, the residuals are not random, a fact that the ingenuity of statisticians has been no more successful in coping with than other unpalatable aspects of observations. The number of observations may not have been large enough compared with the number of systematic factors in operation.

3. Even if the random residuals were small during the period of observation, they need not be so in the future;

then prediction based on the model will be "disproved" in spite of its scientific character. Whether large random residuals in the past destroy the explanatory value of the model is a moot—or rather never-debated—question.

4. The relation between the independent, explanatory, variables and the dependent variable—the one which is to be explained—is always supposed to be of a simple form—a linear, sometimes logarithmic, form. This fact can be explained only partly by the experience of physics in which Aristotle's belief in the superiority of the linear movement was confirmed by hundreds of experimental-mathematical laws. It can be further explained by the pragmatic element in the Western scientific approach which refuses to believe that a few elementary forces by themselves produce a change that can be described only by a complicated mathematical function. Matters are made worse by the fact that any finite observed path of a variable, however erratic, could be explained by some such complicated function, while nobody has been willing to predict the future path by extrapolating such a function. A satisfactory treatment of this problem or of the related question as to the definition of randomness is not known to the writer.

5. Last, but not least, we note the particular extension which the principle of determinism has assumed in social science and particularly in economics. On the one hand, we insist on a one-to-one correspondence between psychological experience (or human acts) and the underlying biological structure of man; on the other hand, we minimize this correspondence, basing explanation and prediction on typical group behavior, observable, but without relation to the biological substructure. This remark does not imply concurrence with the dogmatic criticism of those authors who reject all social science and consider natural science and psychology adequate or at least the only admissible approach. We conclude merely that the

existence of typical group behavior cannot be taken for granted.

It may surprise the reader that, in building a model for the modern economy, we always insist on group behavior functions and seem to deny any particular influence to the individual. And is there not a difference between large groups and small groups? The answer is that, in the present context, the group is not a socially cohesive group, as one considers, for example, the proletariat. In a number of industries there may exist only a few firms, or even only one firm in a monopolistic position; for the case of the few firms there is a special price theory (so-called oligopoly). Nevertheless, unless there is more than one mode, statistical analysis is applicable because we are dealing with the group of all monopolists, or all oligopolists, who are supposed to display a typical behavior with a relatively small mean-square deviation. This typical behavior need not be motivated exclusively by the desire to maximize profit (one of the "idealizing" premises of classicists and neo-classicists), a different typical strategy can be introduced into the model, for example, "expecting the worst," the strategy underlying the famous theory of games.

Even if the defects[61] of the statistical method render impossible a scientific explanation or prediction, the assertor is not likely to become a victim of the ideological fallacies to which a lack of clarity in his concepts, arbitrary un-

[61] As a technical defect, we may further mention the difference between the theory in the natural sciences and the model in economics. Natural forces have an immediate impact, at least on the neighborhood and thus the theories can be written in terms of differential equations. Economic models only seldom can use the concept of a rate of change, which underlies differential equations, because finite periods like the period of production are realities that cannot be eliminated; thus the difference equation becomes an indispensable tool. However, the theory of nonlinear difference equations is far less developed than the theory of nonlinear differential equations. The seriousness of this drawback is indicated by the fact that value, meaning price times quantity, implies the use of nonlinear relations.

tested idealizing assumptions, and faulty reasoning would otherwise have exposed him. He has become a socially unattached intellectual in the investigation of economic events.

E) Equilibrium economics

The concept of equilibrium in this essay is restricted to a state of "rest" or "no change" in the sense that changes are allowed to occur only under the impact of forces outside the model, which sometimes appear in the model as a fixed parameter.

The economics of equilibrium can proceed by examining the dynamic equation system, with a view to finding out whether it will gravitate towards a state of rest; our model does so only for certain combinations of c and v, which are unlikely to materialize. The great schools of the nineteenth century, which dealt with almost nothing but equilibrium economics, used a short cut; they drew conclusions from the idealized behavior of economic units. The case of firms unable to increase profits but willing to stay in business in their present form was expressed by the condition: average costs, including a normal profit, equals price. As a second equilibrium condition, it was stated that all resources looking for employment in the market would be employed. Thus, equilibrium economics stated conditions for equilibrium without being compelled to answer the following questions: How does the economy as a whole act in disequilibrium, and will disequilibrium gravitate towards equilibrium?

8

THE "MODEL" IN SYSTEMATIC SOCIOLOGY

Social science, in general, examines human activities in all fields of action—actions, responses, institutions. Again, it is group behavior, in the sense of typical behavior, which is to be investigated. Explanations and predictions of individual behavior are based on our knowledge of "similar" individuals' actions in "similar" situations. But, as pointed out before, with a view to the individual situation, we may modify observed behavior by understanding.

Our choice of the statistical method as the appropriate procedure may appear surprising because it has never been so used, except in the last twenty years for social relations of a very limited scope. Even in these instances the special interview method was preferred, the establishment of any behavior function was avoided, and conclusions for future behavior were drawn from the pronounced intentions of a sample of the population. However, the verbal reasoning of sociologists concerning cause-effect relations also implies a model in the mind of the sociologist, with "understanding" of behavior playing a much greater role here than in the economics of industrial capitalism. The absence of quantitative measurements in no way excludes the application of modern statistical analysis, not even of crude forms of testing.[62]

[62] In a review article of 1932 (reprinted as Ch. IV of *Essays on Sociology and Social Psychology*, 1953) Mannheim reproached

By way of illustration, we may consider a situation in political sociology. The presence of a "charismatic" leader[63] of a certain type and "strength" (indicated by criteria available before his success), coupled with a well-defined social structure (where the term "social" includes the intellectual approach of the group to social situations) brings about "revolutionary" effects, demonstrable from a number of cases and admitting only a few exceptions of a random character. Both the idealization in the premises and the "weighting" of the social forces are obvious. Another illustration of a deliberately incomplete model (closer to what we called "categorization" as contrasted with "explanation") is contained in Weber's description of bureaucracy:[64] the mere fact of bureaucratic organization does not inform us about the particular nature of its economic effect, though some such effect is always present.

American sociology for its "exactitude complex." He apparently did not see that the statistical method claims only to give answers, not to select the questions to be asked. Nor did he see that Marx's answers to many questions might have been different had he had available statistics about the actual degree (and change) in industrial concentration and accumulation. Mannheim later changed his views. In the posthumous work we find, a little out of context, an almost opposite attitude: "the mastery of the empirical case study method and, in some cases, of statistical sampling procedures is a precondition of sound analysis" (p. 54). It is doubtful whether he ever realized the essentially stochastic nature of any proposition, at least in social science. He could have pointed to the numerous defects of the statistical analysis which we mentioned above, but, of course, if they prevent the fruitful application of the analysis, it is not a sociology of knowledge that remains, but a devastating methodological criticism.

[63] A "charismatic" leader has a quasi-religious position: as a matter of course, his followers consider just and appropriate any action which he chooses. Such leaders appear not only in religion, but also in politics: Pericles, Napoleon (1799-1808), Lenin, Hitler, and Franklin D. Roosevelt were charismatic leaders.

[64] Max Weber, *Wirtschaft und Gesellschaft* (1922), Ch. VI, p. 670.

A) The "historical dimension" of sociology

Sociologists have at their disposal data from much longer periods than have the economists, at least those economists studying modern capitalism. An economic model may suffer changes from exogenous forces every twenty years, and modern capitalism is less than two hundred years old; it is doubtful whether material concerning the European economy around 1700 is of any help in studying the economy of 1960. The comparatively ample material available in many fields of sociology, such as religious or political sociology, is an advantage in suggesting to the scholar where to look, but not always an advantage in building a model which statistically would cover a sufficient number of cases, because the number of variables and relations may increase as the period of observations lengthens. The tendency to restrict oneself to categorization is, therefore, understandable. Nevertheless, although lacking material for adequate analysis, sociologists frequently indulge in causal explanation: one suspects that "ideology" has taken the place of proof proper. Here is one of the roots of Mannheim's skepticism, a basic fact not sufficiently realized by his critics, who took availability of the correct method for granted. Clearly, the misfortune does not have its ultimate root in the inevitable perspective of the scientists, but in his all-too frequent willingness to turn into a nonscientist when the scientific material is inadequate.

B) Political sociology

Sociology, as we now understand the term, was born late in the nineteenth century and first satisfied the basic condition of all scientific endeavor—conceptual clarity—in the work of Simmel and Max Weber. Political sociology, however, goes back many centuries. Its first classic was Machiavelli's *The Prince*. Although the aim of this monograph was to teach a prince how to become a successful ruler, and despite its natural limitations to the Italy of the Renaissance, it presents a model in our sense. Given certain initial conditions, the behavior functions of the political subject and an instrumental variable (the conduct of the princes), it predicts a specific outcome. The term "instrumental" refers to the fact that the typical behavior of princes is replaced by some well-defined required behavior, a replacement that also occurs in certain instrumental models of modern economics, such as the amount of investment necessary to maintain the full utilization of resources, given certain behavior functions and technical relations.

Machiavelli's monograph (and his equally important *Discourses on the First Ten Books of Livy*) remained unique for centuries. Political science or political philosophy became utopian or speculative: from assumed properties of human nature, assumed origins of human government, and ethical norms assumed to be binding, political science undertook to justify or to condemn existing political institutions, and to describe ideal ones.[65] The effect on human history of this kind of writing at times proved tremendous; the outstanding example is Rousseau. But it is hard to see how this procedure could claim to explain what is, or to predict what will be. The place of such work in the intellectual history of mankind is secure, but it is not a part of social science as understood in this essay. Can it be seriously maintained that the "*contrat social*" and the "innocent primitive" are useful concepts in explaining the political reality of any time?

[65] The "Federalist" seems to be the first work in political science which uses again Machiavelli's "pragmatic" approach.

C) *Experiment in social science*

In this essay, sociology has been treated as a nonexperimental science, which analyzes observations expressed in terms of daily life. However, the branch of psychology called "social psychology" is experimental, and although the results are still elementary, it may make important contributions to sociology in the future. Furthermore, it has become clear that psychology cannot, any more than natural science, adequately explain observable behavior without assuming non-observable entities like the "subconscious." Unfortunately, widely accepted theories suffer from the fact that the hypothetized behavior of the non-observable is not uniquely related to particular observable behavior. A theory which is compatible with any possible observation does not explain anything.

In this context we have to mention also the "experimental" process called "simulation" applicable in all social sciences. A process, e.g., of production and distribution (the "firm") is usually at first arranged on the basis of tradition, modified by the ingenious hunches of innovators, which are emulated by other firms and suggest other innovations; much has been learned in the last 100-150 years from the science of nature. The existence of electronic computers, however, opened in the last 15 years new avenues of approach. If it is possible to express numerically the performance of the individual stages in the arrangement, then variations in the arrangement can be examined as to their effect on the overall performance (by varying within reasonable limits the numbers assigned to each stage); at the present levels of mathematics it might be impossible to obtain a *general,* algebraic (non-numerical) solution of the mathematical model that corresponds to the "arrangement."

D) A "total" model in social science

While social science is divided into many fields, man is a unity—a unity which at the same time is able to belong to many "groups." In the economic sphere, he is both consumer and producer; he is also a member of a religious group, a political group, and so on. This overlapping of roles does not prevent a model in economics from having the same man appear more than once in the model. More important is the division into different spheres of investigation: economic activities, religious activities, etc. Events explained in an "astronomical" model of sphere A appear as "exogenous" events, or even as a "break of structure" in a model pertaining to other spheres B, C . . . If we had n such spheres and a model for each of them, so that in each model there appeared endogenous behavior functions and $n-1$ exogenous parameters, explained in the other models, the joining of the models would establish a system that, in principle, and given enough observational material, would be soluble.

There is, however, a defect in this argument. The multiplicity of spheres, which, in principle, we are able to combine in a "total" model reflects the multiplicity of simultaneous activities of man in this world. "Full totality," if this term is allowed, would be reached only if in each sphere the model covered all periods of human history. This is clearly unfeasible not only for lack of material, but also (as we know from the discussion in Chapter 2 of the autonomy of the human mind and, from a different angle, will have to stress in the discussion of historiography in Chapter 10) because of the existence of unpredictable factors in human history, which prevent the establishment of a model valid for all times.

9

EXPLANATORY LAW AND CAUSALITY

As has been pointed out, the discussion of our basic problem in the first part of this essay and the exposition of the procedural rules in the systematic social sciences could be undertaken without distinguishing between empirical explanatory laws and cause-effect relations. Indeed, the older literature was inclined to identify the two concepts, as is evidenced by the frequent use of the term "causal law." Thus, these scholars were led to exclude the directly observable regularities, like day and night, which we exclude because the regularities are not explained and do not aid explanation; hence, it is not possible by the application of statistical criteria to indicate the chance of their persistence.

More recently a number of physicists and philosophers of science concluded that the concept of causality should be eliminated and only the concept of explanatory law should be retained. Surprisingly enough they did not indicate what they meant by explanatory law.[66] Thus some comments on this concept are necessary.

[66] The best discussion we know of can be found in C. G. Hempel and P. Oppenheim, "Logic of Explanation," originally published in *Philosophy of Science* (1945) and republished in part in the *Readings*, ed. by A. Danto and S. Morgenbesser (1960). From the introduction to Part Two of the *Readings* we quote: "And indeed the correct analysis of lawlikeness is an unsolved problem in

A) *The meaning of "Law"*

The generality of our model. That our difference equation represents a law can be denied only by those authors who identify law with indicating the "necessary and sufficient conditions." These terms appeared first in mathematics and have their place only in logical deduction and not in empirical laws. No known empirical law is a sufficient condition for what it explains, because it must be formulated with the explicit or implicit clause: other things being equal. Naturally, the "other things" must be able to remain equal, that is, not be related by a known law to the forces (coefficients) or the substances (variables) in the given law.

Obviously our model can be expanded. In principle, the number of unknown variables can be indefinitely increased, provided the number of equations is increased correspondingly. Furthermore, it is possible to treat the forces appearing in the model either as known functions of the variables or even of time. Only if time itself appears as a variable, as in the time-trends of economists, would the law be incomplete. Otherwise, we call the law complete even though fixed parameters appear or, implicitly, "other things" are assumed to be "equal." Lastly, we note that our model and, indeed, all explanatory laws require the concept of a "substance" (in our model the substance "income") that changes, either in some of its properties or in magnitude or in location. Of course, no general law of conservation of substance is here brought forward. In the following remarks we propose to show that the definition of law implicit in our "model" covers

---

the philosophy of science. We should add that scientists employ the term 'law' more loosely than our set of conditions would indicate."

a substantial number of cases in which this definition does not seem applicable at a first glance.[67]

Laws in which the time variable is absent. Although many physical laws can be written in terms of differential equations, we frequently find laws which do not seem to contain time and do not have the form of our model. Dalton's law reads: a compound is a combination of atoms such that the ratio of the number of atoms of one kind to the number of atoms of any other kind is a whole number. In fact, this law is a prediction of the outcome of an experiment; if different elements are brought together in the prescribed ratio, the resulting compound will absorb them completely. All experiments may be put in a form which relates a state at a given time before the experiment to the state at a later time. The experiment differs from our model in that it is usually not self-perpetuating. This difference is due to the arrangement of the experiment; an outside intervention (a term to be discussed presently) in most cases stops the continuation of the chain of events at a certain time and submerges possible continuations in a larger stream of events generated by other models. Sometimes, of course, a seemingly harmless experiment may ignite the building and destroy the experimenter.

In consequence of this limitation, the symbolical expression of the law is not an equation and there is no question as to the number of unknowns and equations. In this context, the equality symbol has to be replaced by another symbol, say, an arrow, which indicates the process of "production" or "generation." Experiments in chemistry, biology, physics (concerning, for example,

[67] The "axiomatization" of an empirical systematic science is merely one further step in the simplification which we try to achieve by the hypothetical introduction of new "substances" and "forces" of a more general character than the observed ones. The axioms formulate the minimum number of substances and forces

the heat equivalent of mechanical work) yield auxiliary laws, to be eventually inserted into a wider framework.

The interpretation of laws concerning non-observables. The result obtained for experiments with observables is not changed if the model requires introduction of not-directly-observable entities; for these entities have a place in scientific explanation only if their state (which is to be described) and the change in the state are related uniquely to observable events, say A and B. Event A is assumed by the theory to affect a non-observable real entity, sometimes expressed only by a functional symbol or an operator depending on A in a specific way; and this change in the entity, among other things, can be observed as event B.[68]

Behavior functions. A second exception to our concept of law is apparently furnished by expressions such as cY_t, or more generally: consumption is a function of income. What we have used here is an abbreviation. Two cases may be distinguished. In the first case, all consumers correctly anticipate their income, and adjust their consumption accordingly; the anticipation then starts a time sequence, since correctly anticipated income is followed by consumption expenditure, etc. The more likely case is incorrect anticipation on the part of at least some consumers; for this case, it is maintained that, given sufficient time, consumers guided by current information would adjust their consumption outlay, so that

---

required. Any such step away from the realities of daily life is considered more than a brilliant intellectual achievement only if from the more general system new propositions can be derived concerning the observable world.

[68] A very good discussion of the rules of correspondence between "theories" concerning non-observable, hypothesized entities and observables can be found in E. Nagel, *The Structure of Science* (1961) p. 93.

for the whole period the law again is valid; the information on income precedes the action of spending. Thus, behavior functions are a kind of "auxiliary law." A given behavior is explained as the reaction of a group to an event. Having once established behavior functions the social scientists may insert them into a model which states the conditions of equilibrium.[69]

Clearly, behavior functions have a "causal direction," and the event may be termed the "motive" of the action. As we shall see in the next section, to admit a causal direction is not the same as finding "the cause" of an event. Thus Schopenhauer's distinction between motive and cause is more justified than is usually admitted, though Schopenhauer did not obtain clarity about the meaning of "cause."

"Historical laws" and "developmental laws." The term "historical law" is used by G. Bergmann and E. Nagel [70] to indicate relationships not contiguous in time but involving a lag; our model would assume this form if we added on its right side such a term as dY_{t-2}. Hence only differential equation systems, not difference equations, are considered process laws proper; and, indeed, we ourselves denied to time the property of an active factor. Models with time lags, however, can be easily justified in social science: during the period $t-1$, the experience in $t-2$ left its trace in the human mind and eventually emanated as specific behavior. This interpretation would probably be accepted even by extreme behaviorists.

Developmental laws draw conclusions from a given

[69] The establishment of behavior functions from observations of group behavior over time has created particular difficulties (known in econometrics as the problem of identification), because the observations may result from the behavior of several groups, whose reaction to events is so fast that the time interval between event and reaction is not observable.

[70] G. Bergmann, *Philosophy of Science,* pp. 124-130 (1958); E. Nagel, *The Structure of Science,* p. 76.

event for the antecedent as well as the succeeding event. If the given event can be identified with the initial conditions required for full determination in the system of equations these laws are, in fact, identical with process laws; if not, we have no law whatever.

So we may hazard the following brief definition of an explanatory law: it explains a sequence of events in terms of initial conditions and of forces at work, other events being equal.

B) Cause-effect relationships

Cause-effect as disturbance. We invite the reader to look again at our basic model. It undertakes to explain different events, namely, the level of income in periods 2, 3 . . . from the same set of "data," viz. the initial conditions Y and Y_1, and the forces c and v. In other words, the same "cause" has different effects at different times. This is incompatible with the usual meaning of cause and effect, though, of course, the system of operating forces may be called a "causal mechanism."

In actual fact, the difference equation is not only an oversimplified model: the greatest amount of refinement could not protect an economic law against "structural breaks," in the sense of an invasion from other spheres of human behavior. Even astronomy, the one science of nature that is most protected in this respect, is unable to predict the appearance of a nova.

It is these disturbances which are causes; and the difference of the path of the dependent variables after the disturbance from what it would have been except for the disturbance is the effect, although we frequently restrict the term to the first or "most relevant" deviation of the new path from the old.

This definition seems strange because we are scarcely aware of the great number of models describing the "natural" path of events, which are at the disposal of the human mind on the basis of practical knowledge. Thus, if somebody is assassinated, we regard this event as a disruption of the natural path of his life. On the other hand, if we say that somebody died of old age, we do not mean that old age was the cause of his death; we mean, rather, that the path of his life as indicated by the model had reached a certain stage.

Without contradiction, we may consider as cause of the death of Caesar (1) the dagger of envious Casca (disturbance of a biological model); (2) the conspiracy of certain noblemen who did not realize, despite Marius, Sulla, and the events of 59 B.C., that the Roman Republic had lost its indispensable political-social support (the model became invalid) (3) Caesar's negligence in protecting himself (violation of the behavior function of a successful dictator). Obviously, the historian discussing the Roman Republic will stress the second cause-effect relation. The biographer of Caesar may also be interested in the third, but we doubt that any scientist would be interested in the first.

Our formulation differs in some respects from the distinction between a "monocausal" and a "multicausal" approach. Multicausal explanations, unless carefully expressed as disturbances of a model, easily deteriorate into the useless formulation that the state of the universe at a given time is the cause of the state of the universe at a subsequent time. In our approach, any event at a certain time can be conceived as a link in several, but *not innumerable*, relevant processes $P_1, P_2 \ldots$, in the sense that at the moment of time under consideration these processes intersect, so that each process suffers a disturbance or all processes are merged into a new one.

Those physicists who consider the concept of causality

unnecessary and want to limit themselves to the empirical law simply assume that science has reached the state of Laplace's demon[71] who can explain and predict all events from one set of equations and the necessary initial conditions. In fact, science today provides us with an incoherent jumble of laws from which we extract something practically useful. "Even in sciences which are far more advanced than economics like physics there is no universal system available at present." [72]

The alleged asymmetry of explanation of the past and prediction of the future. The distinction between Cause-Effect Relation and Law proves useful for the clarification of a recent controversy, the nature of which can be most easily ascertained from the following question[73]: Why from a limited region of space can we deduce a great deal of history of the past, whereas to predict similar facts about the future even a superhuman intelligence would have to consider initial conditions over a very wide region of space? As illustration we use Robinson Crusoe's indisputable conclusion when he observed a footprint on the beach that had not been there the day before: *in the meantime a human being was on the beach!* But, it is pointed out, while he thus explained the past correctly, he would not have been able to answer the question whether there would be in the future human beings on the beach, i.o.w., to predict "similar" events.

[71] The objections which can be raised against Laplace's concept from the viewpoint of the theory of relativity, or the Entropy concept, are irrelevant for the history of mankind, which is very short in terms of the stellar universe.

[72] Neumann-Morgenstern, *Theory of Games*, 1.2.1.

[73] I was not aware of the controversy until my attention was drawn to it by A. Gruenbaum, *Philosophical Problems of Space and Time* (Borzoi Books 1963), Ch. 9. The question in the text is a quotation of Gruenbaum's from J. C. C. Smart. The following illustration in the text is also taken from Gruenbaum. As far as I can see, there is no difference between Gruenbaum's results and mine, though the approach is not identical.

We note first that Robinson Crusoe in long experience had built up a *model* of the state, or consecutive states, of the beach, in which footprints (except his own) had no place. Hence there was a *disturbance* or *interference* from another model. If this other model (concerning the actions of inhabitants of other islands) had been fully known, Robinson Crusoe would also have been able to predict future footprints. Since practically nothing was known about the other model, also the *explanation* of "the past" was very incomplete. And why should we expect very incomplete explanations of the past to yield much more complete predictions of the future? "Symmetry" means in this context only that when Robinson Crusoe happens at another time to observe a footprint, he will draw the same conclusion as he did the first time. Moreover as we shall show in Ch. 10 (sect. C): explanation by law, valid for past and future, does not imply that an event similar to the event observed at time *t* will ever materialize.

It is not difficult to cite cases in which both explanation of a past event and prediction of a similar event are possible and *based on the same grounds;* e.g., when we observe a train leaving a station today, Monday, at noon, the prediction that another train will do so tomorrow would use the same reasoning as the explanation of the first observation. Moreover, we sometimes cannot explain adequately a past event (e.g., a very cold winter, with a temperature far below the probability range) and yet make a statistically correct prediction of the temperature of the coming winter.

This case will be discussed, in principle, below (Ch. 10, sect. B); already in Chapter 2 an important instance of *asymmetry* was examined.

The cause of an event. In reflecting on an experiment like the generation of water from an appropriate mixture of hydrogen and oxygen, nineteenth century philosophers might have used terms like the following: the initial arrangement, especially the mixture of the two gases, is the adequate cause, the igniting spark is a precipitant and the drop of water is the effect. The distinction between adequate cause and precipitant originates in certain equations in physics and chemistry, such as: 2 atoms *H + 1 atom O = 1 molecule water*. The precipitant, a kind of inferior cause, was sometimes raised to a higher level as in the German adage, "Small causes, big events."

If the distinction between the adequate cause and the precipitant is dropped, then, as has been pointed out, the controlled experiment yields an auxiliary law; but because of the artificial isolation the experiment can also be considered to have established a cause-effect relationship. The attitude of some modern physicists towards causality is therefore understandable: if they have the explanatory law, they do not need the cause-effect relation, which is also represented by the experiment. What they overlook is the fact that they actually have only auxiliary laws, which do not explain the course of the world, in which these laws steadily intersect.

In daily life the impossibility of finding the single cause of an event is well known and the problem is solved by the common sense of the observer who, helped by his practical knowledge, selects the pertinent "natural" path of events which was interrupted by the disturbing cause. For example, if I open my eyes and see another person whom I did not see a few moments before when I closed my eyes, what is the cause? The opening of my eyes, or the entrance of the person, or, possibly, something else? Practical knowledge would suggest the entrance of the person as the cause; but we would modify this answer if all entrances had been blocked.

We conclude, therefore, that the contrast between cause-effect relations in processes and causes of events is a doubtful distinction: except in controlled experiments, where cause-effect and explanatory law are identical, cause is always a disturbance of a natural path of events indicated in an explanatory, "complete" or auxiliary law.

We must conclude this discussion without touching on such famous questions as whether empirical laws and cause-effect relations indicate necessity or only contingency. The question arose because rationalism had confused logical with factual necessity. Likewise we are not impressed by the distinction between laws of nature and mere "empirical generalizations." [74] Can any law that explains reality be obtained without empirical generalization? Is an empirical generalization valid that is not based on laws?

C) *Appendix to chapter 9*

In general, the problem of causality has been treated by philosophers, or more recently by physicists. In the last twenty years there have also been "practicing" social scientists, who have studied the subject in an attempt to distinguish between laws and causation. Some comments on their approaches are in order.

"Social causation." There are parallels between Robert MacIver's approach and ours.[75] MacIver distinguishes between

[74] A thorough discussion of this concept can be found in R. Brown, *Explanation in Social Sciences* (1963), Ch. X. We regret that lack of space does not permit us to comment adequately on Brown's valuable study.

[75] The formulations in this essay are to a considerable extent the result of the studies in economic dynamics, which have occupied me primarily during the last twelve years. It is, however, not impossible that MacIver's book, *Social Causation,* which I read soon after its publication in 1952, and consulted again only after the present manuscript was completed, subconsciously influenced the formulations.

the causation of events, which is "operative in toto" in the occasion of the event, and the causative explanation of a continuous process which cannot be explained by the conjuncture of forces at any one moment but by persistent determinants. It is for the continuous process that MacIver introduces something like our model, and cause as "precipitant"; "the presumption is that a system is operating in a manner congenial to its self-perpetuation, until something breaks it open. The 'something' is a precipitant." (p. 173). In our approach, this notion is extended to the cause of an event, which we can never see except as a phase in one or several self-perpetuating systems. Only in this way is it possible to ascertain as cause "the specific difference between comparable situations" (pp. 63, 123). We may refer here to our remarks on "Comparative History."

Causal ordering. H. Simon, in "Causal Ordering and Identifiability,"[76] was, in our opinion, misled, from the outset by using as starting point the case of a static system. Such a system only establishes the conditions of equilibrium; and in this limiting case we do not need the distinction between cause and effect. Simon considers a "linear structure" causally ordered if it has two components: some "minimal self-contained subsets" (briefly, sets in which the number of equations equals the number of unknowns) and a "remainder," that is, further equations in which, in addition to some of the unknowns in the first component, new unknowns occur. It is easy to see that this approach leads to very curious results.[77] In section 6 of Simon's paper, it is virtually abandoned and, with refer-

[76] H. Simon, "Causal Ordering and Identifiability," Ch. III in W. C. Hood and T. C. Koopmans, eds., *Studies in Econometric Method* (1953), reprinted, together with an older article on causality, in H. Simon, *Models of Man* (1957).

[77] Consider the model: (1) $Y=C(Y)+I$, where all variables are expressed in terms of wage units, and I, denoting investment, is exogenously given; this is a self-contained subset. Relate to (1) the expression $Y \equiv PQ$, where Q is the aggregate net output and P the corresponding price level; in turn Q can be conceived as a function of P and the constant wage unit: $Y=PQ(P)$. According to Simon, equation (1) is the cause and (2) the effect. This cannot be correct. The model states something different: there can be disequilibrium in the market for goods, with prices higher and quantities lower than in short-run equilibrium, while the behavior functions in the first equation is strictly satisfied.

ence to a "metalanguage," it is stated: "the causal relationships have operational meaning, thus, to the extent that particular alterations or interventions in the structure can be associated with specific complete subsets of equations." The similarity to our formulation is obvious, although we are not conscious of having used a "metalanguage," and we do not see why the intervention could not affect all equations. Simon failed to recognize that intervention can originate only outside of the linear structure—in other words, in a different structure or model.

Cause-effect analogous to stimulus-response. In his paper "Causality and Econometrics," H. Wold uses as starting point the controlled experiment.[78] His results would have been similar to ours if the experiment had been recognized as a special case, in which a natural path of events is disturbed by the experimenter. Excluding disturbances in the statistical sense, Wold introduces the regression as the "average causal relationship." We find it difficult to interpret this statement. Is the regression the effect, and are initial conditions and the form of the functions the cause? Or is the regression the cause of the observed events? For nonexperimental observations, Wold considers the dependent variable as effect and the independent variables as causes, without referring at all to the role of time. To prevent the mathematically permissible inversion of dependent and independent variables, he refers to the "explanations of economic theory," which would give information as to what is cause and what is effect. The mathematical possibility of inversion, he points out, is to be kept apart from the question whether causal relations are reversible or irreversible. By a reversible causal relationship Wold may mean a set of consecutive experiments where the state at the end is identical with the state at the beginning; but that is not the usual meaning of cause and effect.

[78] H. Wold, "Causality and Econometrics," in *Econometrica* (April 1954).

PART III

History as social science

10

BASIC PROBLEMS OF PROCEDURE[79]

We do not think it necessary to discuss in detail the fact that all human experience is timebound, and that systematic sciences like mechanics or sociology therefore use the same observational material as does history. Briefly, the systematic sciences discover the laws or models, and the historian applies them in explaining the course of events, although, as we shall see, there may remain very important residues that cannot be explained. The fact that the historian has actually relied, and has had to rely, on his practical knowledge of the laws governing society has been the inevitable misfortune of history, aspects of which we propose now to investigate.

We shall take up first what we may call epistemological problems (A-C), and then the problems arising from the lack of material or in a specific approach (D-F). More precisely our questions are:

A) Which of the almost infinitely detailed events that occurred and are in part recorded enter history as a written science?

[79] Of recent Anglo-Saxon literature I want to mention in particular the thorough studies of P. L. Gardiner, *The Nature of Historical Explanation* (1954) and W. Draxy, *The Law of Explanation in History* (1957). In both these studies the reader will find very convincing refutations of the frequent spurious arguments in the discussion of the essence of history. The main approach in this essay, however, deviates on important points from their expositions.

B) What is the role of atypical events? The analysis of this question will give us an opportunity to discuss a distinction between the tasks #1 and #3 which Parsons outlined for the sociology of knowledge. (See footnote 5.)

C) Can history be considered an individualizing science in contrast to the generalizing sciences of nature?

D) To what extent does the "classical" historical method of source-critique, as developed by Ranke, open the door to "ideological" influences, influences which we now have to define as reflecting the social existence of the cohesive social group to which the historian attached himself?

E) How, in the absence of a "total" model, can history be written as a science?

F) Parsons' problem of "creativity."

A) *Selection of relevant events*

To the best of our knowledge the problem of selecting the events to be described and explained in history from the material available was first systematically discussed by H. Rickert in *Die Grenzen der Naturwissenschaftlichen Begriffsbildung,* first published in 1902.[80] His answer was: History reports what is relevant for the materialization of "values," where "value," like an ethical norm, contrasts with "fact." His proposition did not find universal acceptance, but since grave objections could be raised to alternative formulations, it was accepted by many social scientists, for example, by Max Weber and, if we read correctly, also by Talcott Parsons. The situation is complicated by the fact that, according to Rickert,

[80] H. Rickert, *Die Grenzen der Naturwissenschaftlichen Begriffsbildung,* Ch. IV, Sect. III, 2nd edition, 1913.

these values must have absolute and general validity (p. 352), a postulate which is later reduced to absolute validity in "formal" respects, whatever that means. "If historiography has components claiming more empirical validity we could find them only in the guiding principles of the formation of concepts. But the content of the guiding value aspects of historiography is likewise obtained from objective experience; for the general validity of value—valid as norms for the particular society—as a matter of principle can be established by objective experience." (p. 568). As far as we can see, the sociologists and historians accept Rickert's approach only in the last formulation. In no case would it be justifiable to identify Rickert's value relevance principle of selection with the historian's personal perspective in Mannheim's sense, since in the process of selection the historian is always supposed to be oriented to something which is objectively given to him.

B) *Erratic values*

The statistical analysis of nonexperimental observations is possible only where there are typical systematic forces governing the outcome—forces strong enough to permit us to neglect the random deviations. We thus obtain a model which explains at least the essential course of events during a certain time. This procedure, however, would yield wrong results if and when the highly improbable materializes; in other words, if the random fluctuation becomes so strong that it overshadows the forces in the model, though in the light of experience, we might have been justified in considering the mean-square deviation of the random fluctuation small. We shall call this situation the rise of erratic values.

In the field of economics the erratic values are primarily represented by so-called innovations in technology. The technological horizon existing at a particular time would be changed by the "dynamic" type of entrepreneur, whose innovations are rapidly emulated and the performance of which is in its essence unpredictable, as we pointed out in Part I of this essay. The flow of such innovations may be so strong (although this is not proved) that it becomes possible to assign them a place in a properly reconstructed economic model of the period, thus depriving them of their erratic nature.

But in other areas of social life, especially in political and military activities, the situation is certainly different: erratic values in the past have played a special role under the name of great statesmen, great spiritual leaders, or great generals, provided they appeared at an opportune moment in history and obtained a strategic influence through circumstances largely outside their control. The outcome of the two world wars in the twentieth century conforms with a model which takes account of the relative military and economic strength of the parties; and it does so in spite of Germany's superior general staff—a group of men who, at least in the first world war, had no training in nor knowledge of the nonmilitary strength which ultimately determined the outcome. But this was not always so.

We must limit ourselves to one additional example furnished by the work of Bismarck. The model called the "European Concert" or "Equilibrium of Power" in general operated so as to prevent (1) the unification of Germany, as proved by the events of 1851, and (2) the exclusion of the Austro-Hungarian monarchy from Germany. But, as always, there existed minor factors of random nature offsetting each other in almost all cases according to the law of great numbers. By making clever use of these factors, Bismarck upset, for the time being, the typical operation of the model. But by neglecting the long-run factors operating in the model, especially the rising tide of nationalism outside Germany, and by failing to understand the defects of the political structure which he erected, he also insured its eventual downfall. Nevertheless, in the case of Bismarck, as in the case of Napoleon, some part of his work survived him: the German *Rechtsstaat* (meaning a government checked by a Bill of Rights), which, after important beginnings in the feudal period and under the absolute monarchy, was initiated primarily by Bismarck's liberal opponents, in the period 1848-1878; and the "welfare state," which Bismarck inaugurated in 1880 as a kind of emergency measure, in this case largely over the opposition of the liberal middle class.

For the most part, statesmen and generals have a much better understanding of the forces operating in the foreign policy of their times and of the military forces (although by no means always to an adequate extent) than of the other social forces. In this respect they parallel the case of the historiographers.

Technically speaking, the materialization of overpowering erratic values, even if it fails to change the model itself, does establish new "initial conditions"—and this is equally important. It follows that for history the materialization of erratic values creates an element of unpredictability which cannot be eliminated by any scientific method. Again, explanation is possible, but prediction is not; for history will record the appearance of the erratic values and explain the consequences of this appearance, although science cannot predict them.

Obviously, erratic values of significance cannot be expected to materialize in all periods. In the period 1890-1930 (or 1932) the relevant political-social-historical events can be explained in terms of a model of forces. For we do not regard as cause or disturbance the mere *absence* of great statesmen and generals, who, indeed, might have shaped differently the diplomatic history of 1902-1914 or the outcome of the first world war. The appearance of Mussolini may be considered as a distortion of the particular model valid for Italy, but that country was not strong enough to distort the overall model. For the decades after 1930 Hitler not only established new initial conditions but also transformed the model by radically changing the balance of forces between East and West.[81]

In Part I, we discussed another case of unpredictability arising from what we call the productivity of the human mind. The present phenomenon goes much farther but has different roots: it arises from the limitations of human knowledge, while the earlier case has metaphysical roots. It is also worth noting that while the erratic values are predictable as a possibility with an extremely small chance, and while even their influence on the model may be to some extent estimated in advance, the essential results of the productivity of the human mind are not predictable even as extremely unlikely events.

The preceding analysis treats the great leader only as a "disturbance" or transformation of a model or of initial conditions. But is it not possible for the historian-biographer to understand the great man's personality and the selected complex of mental acts and mental potentialities which we call his motives or his character? Cannot the contemporary observer, having taken note of the great man's actions for some time, predict his actions, or at least their "style"? It cannot be denied that such understanding is possible for the historian or observer; in other words, the great leader becomes a part of the model. More-

[81] A sketch of the models valid for these periods can be found in my article: "Stability in Late Capitalism," *Social Research* (Spring 1954).

over, while the structure of the model operative after the great man has ceased to be active, can often be examined by the historian, without reference to the great man's personality, it would scarcely be possible to predict its modus operandi during his active lifetime solely on the basis of his past behavior, without recourse to "understanding" (*Menschenkenntnis*), which was briefly discussed at the end of Chapter 5. We are, however, not able to say more about this subject, because, so far as we know, there is no systematic "psychological" science on which historian or observer could draw; it is an art, possessed by few; the majority of historians and observers do not even deign to examine the *total* of available records without prejudice.

C) History as an individualizing science

Our basic position is that an adequate explanation in history requires a total model. At first glance, this position seems to imply that history is not the science of individual events, as was maintained originally by Windelband and Rickert and more recently by certain Anglo-Saxon writers. The discussion was unnecessarily complicated by the fact that Rickert could imagine "laws" only as relations between conglomerates of atoms or similar ultimate units of nature. Having made short shrift of this approach, he considered himself entitled to reject all attempts to find regularities in history, without, on the other hand, making clear what *explanation* in history would mean if not explanation by a law according to which a state A is necessarily followed by a state B. The situation was further complicated by the fact that his Anglo-Saxon followers were inclined to interpret history as mere description, while their Neo-Kantian masters rejected the definition of truth as equivalent to a detailed copy of reality.

It cannot be said that the school whose propositions we are examining has been very clear about its concept of individuality in history. Allegedly, the historian is interested only in what distinguishes, say, the particular German Revolution of 1848 from the French Revolution occurring at the same time. But why consider only distinctions between revolutions? These are more or less arbitrary headings under which historians have included the so-called "glorious revolution" in England in 1688-89, but not the struggle between Charles I and the Parliament, or between the Parliament and Cromwell in the middle of the seventeenth century, the so-called "Great Rebellion."

As we shall see, there is no real problem; the discussion was started by philosophers whose understanding of the methods of natural science was inadequate and who were not aware of the overwhelming methodological problems which historiography faced in reality. We shall try to clarify the meaning of individualization by making use of our results.

1. Suppose first that Laplace's demon had done his work for the social world and that an extensive set of equations and initial conditions were available to explain the course of world history so far as the detailed events are relevant. This does *not* mean regular repetition of events. As we see in our model, the same set of forces and initial conditions will produce at different times different historical events—a depression in one period, a boom in another. Thus, with the help of the model, the historian could explain relevant events which look different and are different.

2. It may be argued that, given sufficient time, any model is bound to display one of the following features: (a) recurring constellations; (b) gravitation to a station-

ary state; (c) ever-increasing divergence, with some variables increasing to infinity; Process (c) may be superimposed on process (a). Process (b) cannot be considered as a priori meaningless. Process (a) seems to disturb historians more than some philosophies of the eternal recurrence of all events. The main counterargument will be stated in the next subsection. Here we merely remark that because of the extremely complex nature of a total social model, it is improbable that the recurrence would happen within the lifetime of mankind or even of life itself; thus, in cases (a) and (c), the recurrence would lie outside the validity of the model, in eons when only dead nature and its laws are valid.[81a]

3. The most important factor in this context is the incidence of unpredictable interventions, arising either from the productivity of the human mind, as discussed in Chapter 2, or from what we call the appearance of er-

[81a] In a paper, "When should History be written backwards?" (*Economic History Review*, August 1963), Professor W. Leontief rejects divergent ("unstable") movements as a possible explanation of historical processes, because errors in the initial conditions would result in ever increasing errors in the description of successive periods. Indeed, eventually they would become infinitely large. But it is overlooked that no model in social sciences (except our mythical "total" model) claims validity for all future: we know that the forces at work are bound to change—in our times, say, every 50 or 100 years, for reasons we have discussed before. Neither Professor Leontief nor any economist we know of is disquieted by the fact that the trade volume of the Western world for more than 100 years has increased at an annual rate of at least 3%—a DIVERGENT movement. That such an increase would lead to nonsense if extended over the next 10,000 years is well-known; hence at some time the model must change, a fact which does not necessarily deprive it of validity for current times. It is, indeed, disagreeable that errors in estimating the initial conditions will at some time destroy the applicability of an otherwise correct model; though we are not sure that large errors in estimating the structure of the ultimate stationary state (to which Leontief's preferred convergent movements would gravitate) should have been considered negligible by him. But it is extremely dangerous to explain reality from METHODOLOGICAL postulates. To quote a German satirical poet: "the conclusion is rigorous: that CANNOT be what MUST not be."

ratic values, discussed in the preceding section. We remind the reader that their materialization may not only change the initial conditions of the model but frequently also the model itself. We are quite far from asserting that these erratic values alone are the concern of the historians; on the contrary, their effect cannot be correctly appreciated except within the framework of a model. But obviously, their materialization might prevent repetition or stationariness, even if the model should produce these features in a vastly shorter time than assumed at the end of the last paragraph.

4. In fact, there is no Laplacean demon, even for social life. Social analysis has yielded at best a jumble of models and frequent structural breaks in the individual model, to be explained in a concurrent model. In a sufficiently general model that which would appear as the result of the forces and the initial conditions, now appears as a disturbance. In the absence of a total model, the historian will make much of the individuality of this event. And we should not criticize him too severely for failing to do a job which cannot now or possibly ever be done. We merely wish that the historian would distinguish more clearly between the model of forces prevailing at some time and the changes which either the productivity of the human mind or strong erratic values bring about in a certain period. And we do expect the "individualizing historian" to refrain from quoting the dictum that people who do not learn from history are condemned to repeat it. To repeat it? According to the individualizing conception of history, there can be no repetition.

D) *Source-critique as cause of falsification*

The source-critique has established a set of criteria concerning the reliability of historical sources comparable to the procedure in a court of law. For example, circumstantial evidence is considered more reliable than the testimony of witnesses; firsthand documents, referring to treaties and the like, can be used to gauge the reliability of a witness; the primary source is superior to the secondary source, and so forth. Apparently innocuous, this approach has contributed greatly to bad historiography, since it tended to limit the writing of history to outstanding political and military events (*Haupt-und Staatsaktionen*), the more so since even the historian without special training considered himself an expert in politics. The original documents still extant from an earlier time would record primarily such events as treaties and wars. Thus, one considered as object of, and cause in, history only what was "reliably reported."

In this way, the political ideology of the historian falsified historical writing. The concentration on political-military events was not at all restricted to the school of so-called political historians in Germany, who, at best, relegated other events to a special branch called "economic" or "social" history. To give an entirely different example: in his biography of Gladstone, John Morley, an experienced politician, is at a loss to explain Gladstone's defeat in the elections of 1874 and does not even mention the famous international crisis which started in Vienna at the end of 1873 and spread rapidly over the world.[82] One should remember that even Thucydides,

[82] The same lack of attention to material other than the literary sources which alone exist for the political historian, is also characteristic of the economist C. Brinkman in his *Englische Ge-*

biased conservative that he was, recognized the class struggle as a principal cause of the Peloponnesian War. He, as well as Polybius, had overcome the primitive approach of the "political" historians.

The foregoing remarks must not be construed as an argument for accepting source material uncritically. Again, great help is afforded by learning something about the mental style of behavior, a technique long practiced in philology. Sources have to be gauged as to their reliability, and difficult and dangerous as this part of historiography is by its very nature, mental style may be of great help in evaluating the source.

E) How is historiography possible?

In the absence of a total social model, and of historical material required by such a model, historians who were at least subconsciously aware of the difficulty proceeded in one of three ways, which we may call "Fragmentary History," "Self-Restraint," and "Comparative History."

Fragmentary history. Here biographies of a special type may serve as illustrations. We have already mentioned the difficulties encountered in biographies of statesmen, generals, or successful reformers, which by their very nature become political or military history. We limit ourselves here to biographies of artists or other persons whose influence on the course of history in general and the structure of society was almost negligible during their lifetimes; here the biographer can take the observ-

---

schichte 1814-1915 (1924), p. 127, though in the preface to his book Brinkman proclaims as his intention the coordination of political life and economic structure.

able structure as the datum. Wherever the condition is satisfied, the combination of description and a measure of psychological insight may yield an acceptable biography, although a good history of the time could not be written. In the same way, enough material may be available to explain the winning of a particular battle by one side, while the question why the *war* was won by the one side may not be answerable on the basis of the available material.

Self-restraint. Here we may refer to Ranke's historiography. Nothing is more frequent in his writings than the phrase: "but now this was no longer possible." As his famous essay on the "Great Powers" shows, he always had in mind a model of the forces which, in international conflicts, are decisive, while the actual military encounters are not explained but only described by him. This model clearly would fail in the explanation of other historical events: thus Ranke's *History of the Reformation* is a composite of biographical sketches and the constellation of the decisive international forces for which he had a model in mind. The "domestic upheavals" (*"innere Gaehrungen"*) are registered by Ranke, provided their strength proved sufficiently large; to construct, however, a model weighing these events and relating them to the internationally active forces (let alone to the strength of the religious movement) was not in his power nor even envisaged. Instead trying his hand at a task which hardly could be performed to-day, Ranke developed a philosophy of history by which at least the overwhelming trends are to be "explained": from time to time there appear on the historical scene great "principles" or "ideas" which ultimately dominate the actions of the various groups. But sometimes the principles were in conflict with one another, as was clearly true during the French Revolution.

We do not learn why they arose, whether they are erratic values, or why one of them was victorious.

Comparative history. The comparison of a sequence of historical events with similar events at different times has, first of all, a "negative" task: to refute explanations which historians are prone to give on the basis of rather superficial considerations, if not prejudices. As an example, we choose Gibbon's famous explanation of the fall of the Roman Empire, which he ascribed to the rise of Christianity.[83] We choose it because a new religious movement in its early stages has never modified the system of forces which rule the development of society in the same era. On the contrary, with the exception of Islam, the religious movement itself is likely to be modified by these forces, but the transformation of Christianity in the first centuries, which enabled it to become a "world-religion," is of no interest in this context.

Gibbon is not quite clear about the time during which the Christian preaching of passive obedience is supposed to have exercised its pernicious influence. Not, of course, at all times: as we read in Gibbon's *Vindication,* some time later, "the sense of public and private interest succeeded in reducing the lofty standard of evangelical perfection to the ordinary level of human nature;" in other words, Christians became good soldiers. In general, Gibbon dates the "fall" (as distinguished from the "decline") from Constantine the Great. The events of the fourth century, however, do not support his proposition, since Roman arms were mostly victorious over the barbarians before the battle of Adrianople (378 A.D.); and the valor of the Roman army even in this last terrible defeat (correctly compared with Cannae 600 years before) has never been disputed. On the other hand, to date the fall in the third

[83] Edward Gibbon, *The History of the Decline and Fall of the Roman Empire,* Ch. XXXVIII.

century is impossible, because in its first half the Christian religion was accepted by only a very small part of the population, while martial cults like the Mithras cult flourished; and at the end of the century, when Christians may have made up as much as 20 per cent of the population, the Christian legions were known for their valor.

Gibbon does not understand the forces making for the decline of the Roman imperium over the centuries preceding the fourth. The historian may disregard the destruction of the Italian yeoman by the Roman nobility (from 150 B.C. on, at the latest), because he may consider this basic change deleterious only for the Roman republic, not for the Roman imperium. He cannot disregard, however, the ultimate consequence, viz., the replacement of the Italian soldier by the provincial mercenary, and after the exhaustion of the provinces, by the barbarian. From the time of Caesar, the barbarian component of the Roman army had increased inexorably. The vanishing of the yeomanry as source of military strength, not the "feeble policy of Constantine and his successors," is the reason why after Adrianople, in contrast to Cannae, the replacement of the Roman army from native sources was impossible, and the barbarian became the last military support of the empire.

Nor is the influence of Christianity visible in the other factors making for the decline. The economic strength of the empire had been sapped by the civil wars and barbarian invasions in the third century; the productivity of labor, stagnant over many centuries, declined, while the pressure exercised by the luxury of the privileged classes on the standard of living of the masses remained the same, and that of the military system increased. If those historians are correct who ascribe an unfavorable influence to the transformation of the empire of Augustus and Marcus Aurelius into a dynasty of oriental forms (from Aurelian to Constantine), they point again to a development of pre-Christian origin. The end came because the colonus and slave had no reason to fight invaders whose regime would not be more—in fact was less—burdensome than the Roman regime they had been subjected to for two centuries.

To draw the conclusions from the preceding brief comments: Even where no "total model" in the strict sense is available, the historian, by drawing on all comparable material in history may be in a position to ascertain the role and to weigh the influence of the various factors operative in historical development. The scope of such a "quasi-model" may reach further than Ranke's model of the great powers between 1500 and the French Revolution. Though more embracing than Ranke's approach, however, the approach of "comparative history" will, in general, be compelled (as was pointed out in Chapter 8) to break up the totality of society into various sectors which do not interfere with each other for a long period, though rarely never at all.

Some tentative conclusions. Historical works written by a historian of average qualifications have to be read with discriminating care. The reader has the job of distinguishing between what is description (whose defects the critics will usually point out with acerbity) and what is explanation. There is little doubt in our mind that in the vast majority of cases the historian's judgment, and if not his description, then at least his explanation, was distorted by his prejudices. These prejudices may have originated in hero worship or in a quite inadequate, largely subconscious, model in the mind of the historian. But there are also instances confirming Mannheim. Nobody who reads, say, Sybel's *History of the French Revolution* (the first work on the subject which was mainly built on primary sources) or Macaulay's *History of England* will deny that their prejudices originated at least partly in the ideology of the class in which they had grown up and to which they remained attached. In other cases, we find in place of a model a "psychology" made ad hoc, and not even in accord with the undisputed historical facts; an outstanding example of this was Tacitus, whose *Annals* represent the most inconsistent historiography among the famous works of history known to us. Nevertheless, the literary gifts of the author have, until very recently, convinced the historians who used him as a source; the main exception again is Ranke.

F) "Creativity"

In concluding this chapter, we wish to add some remarks about Parsons' distinction between two tasks of the sociology of knowledge which we mentioned above: to examine (1) the social conditions that maintain scientific knowledge and (2) those which are favorable to "creativity," a term which will prove to be ambiguous. Let us first note that if a level of scientific knowledge characterized by the general acceptance of rules of procedure is once reached and widely enough dispersed, the very application of the methods will, from time to time, create novel results. By novel results, we do not mean those obtainable by rote application of rules or even by any teachable methods. We cannot imagine any social conditions different from those required for Parsons' problem (1) which would make *sure* of (2); but we surmise that as long as (1) is secure, the chance impulses of the human mind will from time to time produce novel results.

There is yet another aspect of the matter. We have discussed the attainment of knowledge by the application of *method*. But there were historical achievements before method was perfected, historical achievements of great suggestive power. They usually made their appearance when the arts flourished; at least in the field of humanistic sciences, they vanished soon after the arts began to decline. Two generations after the death of Euripides and Sophocles, the Hellenic Golden Age ended with Aristotle; and the method, meaning Alexandria and Archimedes, took over. The Renaissance lasted for a similar span, till the death of Tasso and the completion of St. Peter's, and the English Renaissance did not survive for a long period. The multiplicity of nations within the orbit of Western civilization and their receptivity to foreign influences (in contrast to the Roman attitude toward Hellenism) created new renaissances in the northern countries, none of which lasted for a longer period than the original Renaissance; note, for example, the impact on Germany of the baroque in the seventeenth century, and of music in the eighteenth century. Others, like the Scandinavian and Russian Golden Age, lasted an even shorter period. The German Golden Age began in the middle of the eighteenth century for both poetry and the humanistic sciences (long before industrial capitalism started) and it ended before the first world war; Spengler and Gundolf, both born in 1883, are the last names that come to mind.

This is a different kind of creativity and if Parsons wants to explore its social conditions, he has carved out a hard task for himself. Or are those right, perhaps, who, like Goethe and Spengler, insist on a biological analogy in the creative life of nations?

11

A CASE OF IDEOLOGICAL LIMITATIONS

A) Ideological limitations before the nineteenth century

Our problem is the lack of any economic-social theory or history before the nineteenth century. Basic political changes eventually produced activities of the human mind and created a literature, which, in our terminology, would be a part of historical-ideological knowledge. Economic-social changes, of course, would not, in the long run, have gone wholly unnoticed, but theorists rarely showed an interest in them before the nineteenth century, and historians, as we have pointed out, did their utmost to avoid them. The exception is Aristotle's well-known defense of slavery. Even if one accepts the underlying hierarchy of values, his argument had no validity for the later period of Roman finance capitalism, which offered to capitalists sources of income other than slaves tilling the land or working in an ergastulum. The fact that both the new religions, not even excluding Christianity, and the new philosophies avoided the issue presumably would have been adduced by Marx in his uncompleted study of the materialistic conception of history as applied to ancient times.

The explanation of our basic problem can follow various lines. One might say that economic-social changes are gradual, and only spectacular events drew the scientist's attention. If one explains the absence of any systematic investigation by the Romans' general aversion to literature, why is the discussion of these problems, as well as of slavery, absent in the work of Cicero, which is otherwise so close an imitation of the Greek forms of political literature?

Another explanation of a similarly intellectual nature, might contend that, without an empirical model of sufficient scope, the human imagination is unable to anticipate the modus operandi of a basically different economic-social system; essentially this is a tautology, since the terms "model" and "modus operandi" refer to the same processes. The argument gains explanatory value if we remember the rarity of positive additions to practical knowledge during two hundred thousand years of human history. To explain the fight for political power, won by the Athenian but lost by the Roman democracy, appears a simple task when compared with that of explaining any economic-social revolution. Even such powerful minds as Plato and Aristotle cannot be expected to have dealt with all aspects of social life; after all, empirical insights sometimes break into the speculative constructions, for example, the necessity of improving education, the problem of the optimum size of the ideal city, or Plato's analysis of the factors to which leaders like Pericles owed their success. But would it really have required unusual talents to consider a replacement of the slave by the colonus or bondsman, a replacement that actually occurred in later Roman times? Who would deny the influence of economic motives in the opposition to the Gracchian reforms? And if so, why exclude the possibility of similar influences in the political philosophy of the period?

A similar question arises when we consider the century of the Enlightenment. Its spirit is undoubtedly the principal cause of the great reforms of the eighteenth century, but these reforms were considered by their initiators as a correction of abuses rather than an alteration of the social-economic system. Even when great reformers, like

Frederick the Great or Turgot, were at the same time authors, they did not write about their reforms, let alone the necessity of basic economic-social changes. The same era in which Montesquieu started a discussion that was destined to revolutionize within a few generations the political system of the Western world, he refused to discuss even the outworn and almost worthless feudal components of the system, which eventually were swept away by the French Revolution without any basic change in the property concept. It is almost impossible to regard the limits of human imagination as the cause, since at least some of the changes brought about by the French Revolution were seriously considered by reformers, though not systematically discussed before the revolution.

The preceding observations lead to a tentative conclusion: in the absence of a fully developed social science, human knowledge of the existing social system, in the widest sense of the word, *shied away from* a systematic discussion of its economic-social institutions. But this prejudice only set wide limits to the actual discussion in other fields and, far from determining its content in a unique manner, left a substantial latitude of variation which remained independent of any social factors. Enlightenment is not only Voltaire, but also Rousseau, the utopian character of whose writings did not prevent them from being at least as influential as those of his great predecessor.

B) The nineteenth century

Let us test and, if necessary, supplement our tentative formulation by some remarks on the nineteenth century. The economic-social order became the subject of critical scientific investigations, not only in the rising socialistic-communistic literature, but also in the attempts to develop a science of society.

In all probability, the creation and steady economic deterioration of an industrial proletariat generated doubts about the appropriateness of the existing order in the minds of historians and philosophers. However, similar phenomena of deterioration had materialized in earlier centuries—for example, the deterioration of the peasants at the end of the fifteenth century and the impact on real wages of the declining exchange value of gold and silver after 1550. The first event is particularly instructive: deterioration materialized at a time when what we now call the social question could be discussed only in a religious context. After the Enlightenment had separated religious and secular problems, an independent worldly analysis became possible. Again we find the interpenetration of social factors and the development of the human mind, with the mind not exclusively or even primarily governed by social factors.

The socialist-communist critics of the existing economic-social order represented only a small minority of all scholars writing in the same field, but this fact can hardly be attributed to the same kind of "egotistical" aversion that in the preceding century prompted the refusal to discuss the economic-social order. The factors that motivated and influenced an individual author can be revealed solely by the particular biographical study of his life. To surmount bourgeois prejudices nurtured by education and childhood surroundings requires a degree of independence of mind; and the less developed the method of social science, the greater this independence must be. In the field of history especially these independent minds seem to have been the exception.

But in the systematic social sciences, it was precisely the development of method or rules of procedure from the end of the eighteenth century on which, on the one hand, facilitated a critical analysis, but on the other threw into the limelight the ideological components of the socialist-communist movement. A considerable part of this movement was utopian to an extent exceeding even the utopian elements in Plato's State, and could not be considered scholarly work. Marx and his school claimed to have transformed the communist approach from utopia to science. For various reasons, this claim was not convincing to a critical scholar. Marx's theory of exploitation was clearly a distortion of the Ricardian labor value theory from which it claimed to be derived. Moreover, the collapse of capitalism is explained in Marx's theory by his law of increasing misery of the masses, a law whose empirical invalidity had already become visible in the seventies. The invalidity was partly acknowledged by Engels and represented the starting point for the revisionist movement, which in the first decade of the twentieth century gained complete control of the socialist parties in Germany and France. Further, as pointed out before, the speed of concentration of enterprise and the size of the accumulation of capital, indispensable to Marx's theory of the collapse, were grossly exaggerated. And finally, even if Marx's work could have been acknowledged as a fully satisfactory analysis of the capitalistic forces, the transition to communism was still described in utopian terms as a "Leap into the Realm of Freedom," a concept which created immense difficulties for the Marxist party in Russia when it came into power in 1917.

Thus, apart from the rise of a scientific sociology, we find in the second half of the nineteenth century two important tendencies. First, classical economic theory was thoroughly reconstructed, and the work of the reconstruction dominated Anglo-Saxon, Austrian, Italian and eventually French thinking. It was of such great magnitude that it diverted the energies of the human mind from the critical analysis of the economic-social order as such.

The second tendency appeared primarily in the German historical school. We are not interested here in its misguided effort to deny validity to any theoretical construction, but in the school's social criticism, sometimes called "professorial socialism" or "social welfare liberalism," in contrast to the Manchester liberalism which it opposed. In the present context, the positive economic program of the German school is of less significance than the methodological approach. As a study of its principal works, especially G. Schmoller's *Grundriss,* would convince the reader, we have to deal here with a serious —as we would say, sociological—investigation of the forces operating in society. The main defect, which caused the collapse of the school during the first world war, was the failure to recognize that not only the rational economic theory of the industrial age, but all social science, has to operate with idealizing models in which the typical processes play the central role.

Although after the death of Engels, Marxism rapidly disintegrated into a kind of worldly "theology," quarreling over the true meaning of its "classics," the "bourgeois" social science created new instruments of analysis like communication theory, activity and operational analysis, and so on. Most of these tools are of equal importance for a collectivistic or a capitalistic economy; they are partly utilized by the communist countries, as are bourgeois mathematics, science and technology. This confirms our proposition that it is the *good method* which, eventually, creates the perspective-free intellectual. We are far from maintaining that the process is completed and we have indicated reasons why in a field like history the process has scarcely begun. But we feel justified in maintaining that we have come a long way since the end of the eighteenth century and have entered a new phase.

There is no indication that the social scientist uses his liberation from perspective, provided by the rise of good method, outside the field of his special study. And we have no reason whatever to assume that even in the Western world the bulk of mankind, which has at best a mere technical knowledge and no scientific training, is in any respect freer from perspective than the Athenians in the times of Pericles. This is not surprising. A methodologically satisfactory treatment of the social sciences in general is just emerging. It will be a long time before it is completed and generally accepted, and before it transforms the system of education (below the college level), which, except for a very inadequate introduction to rudimentary social sciences and some more important pedagogical reforms, is not much different from the system which has been in existence for many a century. Since much of what it taught and learned by the average pupil will be rapidly forgotten and never used in his life, we cannot predict, for the present at least, that better education in methodologically sound social sciences will really alter man.

In any case, if the intellectual history of mankind up to the present time should ever be written in terms of good method, we fear that the pressure of the social environment will not prove to have abated in the five to six thousand years which we call the era of higher civilization.

Appendix 1

THE MATERIALISTIC CONCEPTION OF HISTORY

The vagueness of the famous Preface to Marx's *Critique of the Political Economy* (1859) has been frequently pointed out (see, for example, Thomas G. Masaryk, *Grundlagen Des Marxismus,* III A). Much of the vagueness vanishes, however, when we realize that Marx expresses here, in terms applicable to all history, his views about the essence of industrial capitalism and its inevitable development, a purpose for which the *Critique,* later baptized *Das Kapital,* was written. Read, for example, in place of ". . . production structure that corresponds to a certain stage of development of the material forces of production . . ." the simpler statement: "relationship between proletariat and capitalists which corresponds to the way in which in the age of manufactures, of the steam engine and the machine tool, the productive resources were used." Four sentences later read: ". . . beginning with the 17th century and especially around 1800 the use of resources as peculiar to the preceding feudal era becomes incompatible with the innovations in production, including agricultural innovations. A social revolution breaks out. In analyzing such revolutions we have always to distinguish between the changes in the economic condition of the production (which can be ascertained by methods as exact as those of natural science) and the ideological forms in which man becomes aware of the conflict and resolves it by fighting. These ideological forms are legal [change from "status" to "contract"], political [parliamentarianism in place of absolutism or rule of the estates], religious [changeover to enlightenment, agnosticism, atheism], artistic [the new realism of Balzac and Semper], philosophical [the replacement of scholasticism by the British empiricists, the continental rationalists, including Kant, the formulation of dialectics by Fichte and Hegel, the reformulation of dialectics, under the influence of Feuerbach, by Marx and Engels]."

Marx then extends this scheme to the earlier production structures. He would probably have explained the relations between landowner and bondsman or serf, and between master and journeyman or apprentice, from the production methods of the feudal period. But he would have found great difficulties in extending the scheme to ancient times: in ancient times unchanging methods of production were associated with political forms as different as the Greek polis and the principate of Augustus; with religious forms as different as ancient polytheism and early Christianity; artistic forms as different as the Babylonian, Egyptian, and Hellenic arts; philosophical forms as different as the Greek speculation from Thales to Aristotle and the ethical theories of the Stoa.

Even more important is another point: in the Preface the revolutionary changes in the use of material forces are not explained. An answer to this question can be found in the posthumous work of Marx and Engels entitled *Deutsche Ideologie,* written in 1845-1846 and published in Germany in 1932. The first section under the heading "Feuerbach" gives a survey of the history of mankind from the viewpoint of production, and contains the first presentation of the materialistic conception of history (see p. 27). Concerning our present problem, we read on p. 59: "In the development of the production process eventually a stage is reached on which productive processes and means of transportation materialize which in the given circumstances only create disaster—which are powers of destruction (machinery and money)." It is not clear whether the authors refer here to an accidental process, or unexpectedly allow the human mind a certain autonomy of development, production possibly representing the "thesis" and destruction the "antithesis."

Engels' well-known later modifications[84] need only few comments. By replacing Marx's earlier formulations with the all-embracing concept of a mutual interaction of economic and ideological factors, he conceded practically everything to the critics. He reverts, in some measure, to the earlier formu-

[84] Reprinted in L. Woltmann, *Der Historische Materialismus* (1900), II, 4 Sect. 6.

lation by insisting that the secular trend of the ideological development runs parallel to that of the economic development. Apart from the lack of an explicit causal relationship in this formulation, the course of ancient history suffices to deprive this statement of general validity.[85]

In his last modifying letter of 1894, Engels deals with the influence of "great men" in the following way: "if, in a thought experiment, we eliminate the great men who actually appear, there would be a demand for something that replaces them, and this replacement materializes *tant bien que mal,* at least in the long run." Engels completely overlooked the fact that the historic moment at which what we called the erratic value materializes is of decisive importance. Had Napoleon been born in 1779 instead of in 1769, the course of world history would have been different, since among the other generals of the French Revolution there was none who could have taken his place. Another example: it is widely recognized today that, had Lenin been prevented from leaving Switzerland, Bolshevism would not have triumphed in Russia.

The reference to ancient history is also sufficient to show that Marx's materialistic conception, as expounded in the Preface, is not identical with the famous thesis in the Communist Manifesto: "all history is the history of class struggle." The class struggle in ancient times, between plebs and patricians, nobility and yeomen, slave and master, was not associated with any change in the methods of production.

Here the ambiguity of the terms "production relations" or "productive power" again is evident. The replacement of the Italian yeoman by the latifundia transformed Italy from a grain-producing country into a country raising livestock. Both forms of production had been known for thousands of years. Thus, the replacement was not a new technological development; it has to be explained and cannot serve as a basis of explanation.

On the whole, the formulations in the Preface are the most radical ones. Not only did Engels soften them afterwards, but in the *Deutsche Ideologie* we find a surprising statement

85 The rather mysterious distinction between production as "ultimately" determining history and "solely" determining it is not discussed here. "Ultimately" is the translation of the German term "*in letzter Instanz,*" originally a legal term referring to the judgment of the highest court, from which appeal is not possible.

about the possible "independence" of legal forces from productive power (p. 52). "The state is autonomous today only in those countries where the estates have not yet been transformed completely into classes . . . , where, therefore, no part of the population can dominate the rest." It seems that Marx, who began as a philosopher *and* revolutionary, lost more and more interest in philosophy when he took up economics and did not bother much to formulate his philosophy of history in greater detail.

Appendix 2

A SURVEY OF THE PROCEDURAL RULES IN THE SOCIAL SCIENCES[86]

A) *Epistemological presuppositions*

1) The principle of a world fully determined by laws is modified by acknowledging the probability limitations of the cognitive process; measurement is never quite correct and the operation of a great number of forces, not accessible to observation, has to be accounted for by admitting the possibility of random deviations of a size unknown for the future.
2) The degree of errors admissible in explanation and prediction is determined by the risk which mankind is willing to bear in the application of the laws.
3) The existence of random deviations sets a limit to the correctness of prediction and possibly induces man to choose for his behavior strategic rules which would allow him to counteract undesirable effects of the random forces.
4) The cognitive activities of the human mind, conditioned as they are by social forces and by its own history, contain an element which is unpredictable as to essentials, but understandable retrospectively.

B) *Rules of procedure*

1) To explain past events in the social world and to predict future events, we understand this world as a system of forces, representing typical group behavior. In a complete explanation only random deviations in the model based on the behavior functions and natural forces are permissible.
2) The individual belongs to various groups at the same

[86] The defects of the statistical analysis are not summarized in the survey.

time; thus, in any partial model, "exogenous" influences appear, originating in possibly unknown outside models. In principle, however, all partial models can be integrated into a "total" model, which, except for the point made under the first presupposition above, would furnish a complete explanation and allow prediction as to essentials.

3) "Essential" events of social life are those events that contribute to the materialization of cultural values acknowledged as valid by the majority of people in a civilization for which the model is established.

4) Models are established by the following steps:

a. Selection of essential events.
b. Construction of tentative models on the basis of practical knowledge of the structure of society; the symbols used in the model must stand in a one-to-one correspondence with the relevant events or types of behavior.
c. Measurement of the behavior functions appearing in a model on the basis of observation.
d. Selection of the definite model by statistical tests.

5) Observance of these rules of procedure liberates the investigator from the one-sided "perspective" imposed on him by nonscientific attitudes of the group to which he belongs by birth, education, or other circumstances. Empirical observation shows that only few individuals succeed in liberating themselves completely in all intellectual and practical activities.

6) In addition to the unpredictable effects of the productivity of the human mind, there may materialize atypical or erratic events, which as such have a very low probability; so-called "great men" belong to this category. Their materialization may affect the model itself, or it may affect the "initial conditions," starting history on an unpredictable track which can be recorded and to some extent understood retrospectively.

INDEX

Page numbers in italic indicate the principal place or places where the author or subject is discussed.

H ON THE SOCIOLOGY OF KNOWLEDGE
an essay

The text is set in Linotype Primer, an extremely well-proportioned and readable type face designed by Rudolph Ruzicka and cut by Linotype in 1951.

The display face used on the title page and part titles is Monotype Perpetua, one of Eric Gill's many contributions to typographical design. Perpetua was cut by Monotype in 1929.

The book is printed by letterpress on a Glatfelter antique stock, with composition, printing and binding by H. Wolff Book Manufacturing Co., New York.

Design: Adrianne Onderdonk